OL' DOC'S
CORNFIELD CHRONICLES

featuring
SNOWBALL -
PONY FROM HELL

To Sherri:
Great to meet you.

Myron Williams

OL' DOC'S

CORNFIELD
CHRONICLES

featuring
SNOWBALL -
PONY FROM HELL

by

Myron Williams

Illustrations by Blair Gauntt

All Writes Reserved Publishing

2017
All Writes Reserved Publishing

Design, layout and cover art
by Blair Gauntt

ISBN-978-1-97999-605-1

website
www.mlwilliamsbooks.com
email
mlwilliamsbooks@gmail.com
social
twitter.com/mlwilliamsincr
pinterest.com/mlwilliamsbooks
instagram.com/ml_doc_williams/

Table of Contents

Acknowledgements

Two people have been vital to the production of this book: Blair Gauntt, who designed the cover, created those great illustrations and was in charge of production; and editor Ron DeChristopher, friend and former colleague, who "polished" the copy to help make me sound somewhat coherent.

Also, my family, friends, former classmates and neighbors have encouraged me and been very supportive of this project, which sort of took over my life for most of this year. Even strangers have offered kind words when they found out about this collection of short stories relating to my experiences of growing up on an Iowa farm.

To all of you — thank you so much.

Myron Williams

Dedication

To the ghosts of all those people who came
back to help me relive some precious moments.
Except for Snowball.
I hope she is burning in pony hell.

Introduction

Growing up on a farm can be a special experience. It can be hard at times because parents expect kids to start helping at an early age. But, it also can be a great playground, a place of adventure and space to wander.

I wrote this collection of stories as a way to share memories with my children and grandchildren. To relay some of my childhood experiences on an Iowa farm that was in our family for more than a hundred years.

Snippets of some of these stories could be shared around the dining room table or during visits, but life sometimes gets busy with harried five-minute conversations, texts, emails and computer/smart phone face time.

Writing this collection has been a way for me to bring back family and friends who have passed on but remain very vivid in my memory. It's my way of ensuring some of their stories will live long after I join them.

Quite a few folks in these stories, who are close to my age and younger, are still alive. I hope I have treated them well and that they enjoy my meanderings down memory lane.

Most of the stories take place from the late 1950s to early 1970s. This is the telling of one boy's experiences (mine) on one Iowa farm at one point in time. It doesn't reflect other farm kids' experiences. It is not supposed to. Every farm and every family is different.

I tried to avoid using offensive language but a few words — fairly mild by today's standards — have been used in a few of the stories. It's a rare person who can work in sweltering summer heat during haying season or have an animal turn on them and not utter a perfectly descriptive off-color phrase.

An old farmer once helped pull hay bales off of yours truly after a stack collapsed on me while baling. I was not hurt but came out of the pile swearing like a sailor. I apologized to him for my potty mouth.

He just chuckled, helped brush me off and said, "It's OK to swear, son. Never trust anyone who doesn't swear. They've got something to hide."

Some of my family and friends might be puzzled by seeing me referred to as "Doc." No, I did not go back to school and earn an advanced degree. It's not deserved, more like christened. After retiring a few years ago from a career in journalism, I turned my attention to fiction writing and used my initials — M.L. — for my author name.

During a book-signing event with other authors, a local newspaper misprinted my name as M.D. in a news item. After that, I joked I should be called Doc. Guess what? The other authors started using the nickname, and the moniker stuck.

The farm boy stories are told as I remember them. Some are humorous, others nostalgic, and one is brutally honest. Most are about my adventures and misadventures. The conversations are reconstructed to the best of my memory and reflect most likely what was said at the time. I may have applied some "artistic" license, but not much.

Some of the experiences were traumatic, humorous or sad and were burned into my brain. Writing about them has helped me relive those moments.

If these stories revive memories in others who read this, I hope they are pleasant ones.

1
County Fair

It's county fair season at this writing — July 8, 2017. What better time than to remember my glorious and inglorious moments from the one time I showed hogs 51 years ago at the Hardin County Fair in Eldora.

Mom and Dad weren't much into all the hoopla and preparation that goes into showing animals at the fair. My three brothers broke them in, however, with their "baby beef" 4-H or FFA projects years earlier.

I remember seeing pictures in family albums of them grooming mid-size Angus and Hereford steers and later discovering a colorful assortment of ribbons.

Joining 4-H and later FFA (Future Farmers of America) was not an option for most farm kids. It was expected.

Even though my family members were not that active in the community, 4-H and FFA were a tradition. A lot of my town buddies were in Boy Scouts but my folks were not overly enthusiastic about my entreaties to join a troop.

So, at age 10, I joined the Hardin Township Stockmen 4-H Club. This was the boys' group, which focused mainly on showing livestock. Girls were welcome to join the club, and they often bested their male counterparts in the show ring.

At that time, the girls had a separate group if they participated in non-livestock events. The clubs since have melded into one group for both sexes. I believe the closest club to my old stomping grounds is called the Ellis Jackson Ag Stars — cool name.

Several years after I joined, my club decided to pool something called "sow bucks" and use them to purchase a gilt (young unbred female) for one of the members. I believe the sow-buck program was run something like coupons or the old S&H "Green Stamps."

You collected a tag or a buck from a sack of a certain kind of feed. Once you collected enough bucks, you could take them to a hog breeder to buy or get a discount on the purchase of a hog.

Forgive me, but the lapse of 50 years has clouded my memory how I got to be the sow-buck recipient. Perhaps my name was drawn out of a hat or I volunteered, which seems a bit unlikely but you never know.

My 4-H leader at the time was a Duroc breeder. He offered to redeem the bucks for one his auburn-colored gilts. The female then was shipped to another Duroc producer who bred her to one of his boars.

Three months, three weeks and three days later (I'm not totally sure about the accuracy but that's the average gestation period for a hog), my 4-H litter was born. The litter of six piglets was evenly divided between three boars and three gilts.

I should have called the boars Moe, Larry and Curly after the famous Three Stooges. Moe was the dominant male and sported a perfect, well-muscled body. Curly was thickly built, carried a bit more fat and moved slower. Larry was the smallest of the three and even was lighter in color.

It was unusual to see such a variance, the litter mates got fed the same ration. I made sure all had enough to eat. Maybe Larry got shoved aside to a poor-performing teat when they were piglets.

The sisters could have been triplets. I could not tell them apart. The gilts all were sleek, the same size and looked to have the right characteristics to be good mothers. They were mirror images of their mother.

A month or so before the county fair, we picked out four of the litter mates — Moe, Curly and two of their sisters — to take to the fair. At that time, the hog show allowed litters of four to be exhibited as a pen. Moe and one of the sisters were entered in their respective boar and gilt shows. Due to disease concerns, purebred swine no longer are exhibited at fairs.

Moe was the obvious choice to go into the ring for the boar show and whichever female happened to be closest to the gate was the entry for the gilt show. Being a rookie exhibitor, I did not know what to expect but got a few tips on taming and training the four fair-bound hogs.

Whenever I walked into their pen to feed them, I patted them to get them accustomed to being handled. I even guided them around using light taps from a walking cane. There was no way to prepare for what happened in the show ring.

On entry day, we got to the fairgrounds early in the morning and unloaded our hogs into one of the pens in the swine barn. The pens were roomy enough and my hogs gave their neighbors on either side of them the traditional nose-inspection greeting.

Being a first-timer, I had no idea as to the ins and outs of the county fair. Luckily for me, an older exhibitor who lived only a few miles from our farm — Darwin Miller — took me under his wing and showed me the ropes. Thanks, Darwin. You made a stressful time a little easier for a 13-year-old rookie.

Darwin must have been destined to be helpful. He is the current Hardin County Extension Director and oversees the many programs, including 4-H, that offer worthwhile services to folks in the rural and town communities.

The Duroc show was scheduled for 9 a.m. the next day. On show day, I arose with butterflies in my stomach. They fluttered faster and got bigger as it neared the time to step into the show ring.

It didn't help that I had a jeering section. Yes, jeering not cheering. Three guys about my age from Eldora spotted the nervous exhibitor from Iowa Falls and had fun giving me their opinion on my lack of showmanship abilities.

At the time, folks from Eldora and Iowa Falls didn't like each other much. According to folk lore, in the late 1800s some Eldora hooligans stole papers that designated a county seat from a safe in Iowa Falls and absconded with them back home.

The folks in Eldora later used those papers as proof their little community was the rightful county seat. For some reason, they won the argument in court — as the old saying goes: "Possession is nine-tenths of the law."

The county courthouse was built in that quaint little village as opposed to the prosperous and burgeoning metropolis that was to become Iowa Falls — The Scenic City.

Yes, I am exaggerating the shortcomings of Eldora and accomplish-ments of Iowa Falls. I am hoping to score a free hot beef sandwich and/ or chocolate malt with sidecar from the Princess Cafe via the Iowa Falls Chamber of Commerce.

Of course, the good folks in Iowa Falls were righteous in their indignation and a feud was born. It also didn't help during my time in school that Eldora had really good football teams that joyfully pummeled our Iowa Falls Cadets for several years.

That changed my senior year, when the Cadets stomped Eldora on their home field. I had never seen our high school principal smile so much before or after that victory.

17

On my school bus ride home, the trip often coincided with an El-dora bus arriving at the same time at a gravel road intersection. The drivers usually exchanged friendly waves, but the nasty little kids in both buses rushed to the windows and shouted rude opinions about the others.

Right before I stepped into the ring, one of my fellow 4-H club members dropped this tidbit on me.

"See that girl over there? Her hogs were sired by last year's Minnesota State Fair boar champ. They say he's worth $1,000."

Now, that didn't help my nerves one bit.

The gilt show was first. I guided my sleek little Duroc into the pen and steered her around the ring. She and the other females curiously looked each other over but meandered peacefully, inspecting the ring.

I was making rookie mistakes like putting myself between the judge and my hog which blocked his view. My jeerers loved it and let me know about it.

However, as we corralled our gilts for the judge's final inspection, I noticed something had changed. It was quiet in the jeering section. Not a peep. I looked over to see Darwin and one of his friends sitting on either side of my "fan" club. The Eldora kids looked a little meek. Thanks again, Darwin.

The judge made his decision. The daughter of Mr. Thousand Dollars was selected as champion, and my gilt got second — scoring me a blue ribbon.

The judge said it was a tough decision, but the winner "carried herself just a bit better." I had no idea what that meant but was OK with that.

My nerves were settling down now. This showing thing wasn't that bad, just let the hogs wander aimlessly and stay the heck out of the judge's way. Oh, that wasn't even a warm up for what lay ahead in the boar show.

Guess what ensues when you put six alpha boars into a show ring at the same? Mayhem! The boars exhibited none of their sisters' calm decorum. They rushed toward each other, including my Moe, and start growling and fighting.

Of course Moe had to take on the son of Mr. Thousand Dollars and soon the two were pushing and biting at each other. Froth from the boars' mouths was flying everywhere. Boar scent filled the air.

None of the other exhibitors, including myself, could control the rumble taking place in the show ring. In a flash, all the dads rushed in, grabbed wooden show panels and tried to separate the combatants. All we exhibitors could do was stand aside and watch the mayhem that was going down.

The judge finally stepped in and told everyone to corral their hogs. He would evaluate them from the enclosures. After several minutes of walking back and forth to examine the contestants, the judge was ready to make his announcement.

He said it was another tough decision. "Uh, oh," I thought. "Another blue ribbon isn't too bad."

The judge went on to explain the boar he was looking for should possess "a good, well-muscled carcass that can be passed on to his progeny. And, he should possess the vigor to stand up to the rigors of being a sire."

I was looking down at the saw-dust covered show ring, getting ready to force a smile for coming in second, again, when a hand stuck out in front of my face and interrupted my thoughts.

A smiling judge was standing in front of me. "Congratulations, young man. Your boar gets the purple (champion ribbon)."

I stood there, stunned for a moment, shook his hand and hopefully mumbled "thank you." It was a surreal moment. The few people in the stands applauded, even the Eldora kids.

I looked over at the girl who had showed the son of Mr. Thousand Dollars. She had stuffed her second-place blue ribbon into her back pocket and was hurrying her boar back to his pen in the barn.

The judge later looked over the litters in their barn pens. He handed me the second-place blue ribbon and told me I had a nice looking group of pigs but Curly — my second boar — was a bit too heavy for his liking, which interrupted the consistency he'd like to see. The litter of Mr. Thousand Dollars was awarded the purple.

That was the end of my livestock-showing career. The free-for-all in the show ring probably frazzled Dad more than he'd admit, and I'm sure he was not eager for a repeat performance. Besides, I had scored a purple and two blue ribbons and was ecstatic with that because I remembered seeing a lot of red and white ribbons among my brothers' collections.

Later that summer, Moe and Curly were sold to one of Dad's friends. They were used as sires to produce market pigs. Early the next year, an ad appeared in a local paper: "FOR SALE: Top-quality weaned feeder pigs sired by the Hardin County Champion Duroc Boar and his brother."

In payment for feed and other expenses, Dad used Larry as a sire for our market hogs. He got a little bit bigger and took to his duties with great gusto. His progeny received high grades for their quality carcasses.

As part of my 4-H club's sow-buck reciprocal agreement, we gave my blue-ribbon gilt to one of my fellow 4-H club members. The following year, one of her sons received a blue ribbon at the county fair.

We borrowed a purebred Duroc boar to breed to my two remaining gilts. I sold their sons and daughters for purebred stock for several years and got a nice boost to my college fund.

2
The Guardians

People often ask why I don't I have a dog. Well, for one thing, I now live the city which means a dog would take a lot of care and attention.

My canine friends were farm dogs — valuable assets to our family. They barked at strangers, slept where they wanted, came when called, only wanted occasional attention, chased off intruders (usually four legged) and pooped in out-of-the-way places.

Another excuse I use is that after three children and now six grand-children, I don't want another critter scampering around.

However, the main reason I haven't had a dog since leaving the family farm is that I've had two special dogs in my life — Charlie and Ben. How do you replace two members of your family? You don't.

The following is fondly written in tribute to those loyal pets.

~ Charlie ~

As long as I can remember, my family always had a farm dog. My first memory of a dog is a growling beast that would snap at me when I started going outside to play by myself. The dog (it's name may have been, Shep) was accustomed to adults, not a four- or five-year-old who just wanted to play in the yard and pet it.

After a summer of watching the dog grow increasingly irritated toward me, it became obvious something had to be done. I never found out what happened to it, but one day the dog was gone. I suspect Mom was not pleased at not being able to trust it with her youngest son. Trouble animals on the farm sometimes have a way of "disappearing."

Maybe a year later, Charlie appeared on the scene. One summer day, my brother, Gail, drove up to the house and yelled for me to come see something. I ran over and watched him open the trunk of his car and pull out two plump, fuzzy puppies. They were about three months old.

One was a black-and-white female and the other was a male, pure white except for his head which was a pretty golden brown. Gail said the pups were from a neighbor. He told me to pick one and he'd give the other to a friend.

I sat down on the ground and watched the pups as they sniffed around. The female shivered with fright and huddled at Gail's feet. But, the male scampered over to me and crawled into my lap.

Decision made. "I want this one," I announced.

"He looks like Charlie Myers!" my irreverent brother joked as he held up the new addition to the family. The pup had a long nose probably due to some collie ancestry. The name stuck.

Charlie Myers was a neighbor who farmed a couple of miles away. He and Dad often helped each other out when an extra hand was needed with baling or corn shelling.

Charlie, the neighbor, actually was one of the nicest, gentle and most soft-spoken people I have ever met. He and his wife, "Goldie" (Golda, actually) did not have children and always were kind to the smart-aleck Williams boys. I'm not sure why Gail picked on Charlie, but he thought naming the pup after him was a good joke.

We had to be careful when the neighbor came over to work when Charlie the dog was around. If we had to address the dog, Dad would call him "Shep," and I just said, "Here, boy!" Both Charlies got along just fine. Hopefully, Charlie the neighbor never suspected his namesake was wagging its tail at him.

About the same time as the new pup arrived on the scene, a young tom cat claimed our farm as his territory. The two new arrivals basically ignored each other until one day when Charlie decided to chase the tom — bad idea. The pup charged the cat. Instead of running, the feline dropped to its back with feet up in the classic cat defensive position.

Charlie ran into four heavily clawed paws that slashed at him unmercifully. The pup yipped in pain, turned and ran to me. Blood oozed out of scratch marks all over his muzzle.

The cat got up and stretched. His tail was swishing back and forth like an angry snake. With the battle for king of the farm decided, the tom turned and sauntered back to the barn.

This was the first and last time Charlie ever chased a cat. The tom (cleverly named Tommy) and the dog eventually declared a truce and tolerated each other.

We never knew what bloodlines were represented in Charlie. He was unusually marked with his brown head and all-white body. Charlie looked a bit like a collie with his shaggy hair, but he was shorter and more thickly built. His thick tail curled up only when he was in a defensive posture.

Charlie served his calling as guardian of the farm admirably. No vehicle drove in without him barking a warning. He usually kept sounding the alarm until one of us yelled, "Shut up for Pete's sake" or until he greeted the visitors with a furious tail wagging. He never snarled or snapped at anyone.

While my dog never learned to round up cattle or hogs, good ol' Charlie saved me a couple of times from being trampled and kicked. One of my chores was to bring the cattle back to the farmstead after they'd spent the day grazing in a pasture about a tenth of a mile a way.

Most of the time, this job went off without a hitch. The cows and often a lone bull would be huddled by the gate, wanting to get back to the lot and drink from the stock tank. With a command of "sic 'em," Charlie would bark at the herd until they backed up enough for me to unfasten the gate and get out of the way.

Once in a while, a lone cow with a new calf or spooky heifer would take off for the far end of the pasture. This usually never turned out well. I had to make sure the rest of the herd was headed in the right direction, follow them up the road, shut the gate to the lot and return to the pasture to get the truant critter.

It was a good thing Charlie always went along with me. One time, a new bull was being uncooperative about leaving. I walked behind him, giving him a lot of space and started driving him toward the gate which opened to the road.

I made the mistake of getting between the bull and the fence where I could escape over or under. The bull snorted, pawed the ground, bellowed once or twice and charged me. I backed up, terrified, knowing I could not make it to the fence on the other side of the pasture.

A white blur shot past me and attacked the bull. The creature spun around to face Charlie who circled him and snapped at his legs. After several minutes of "playing chicken," the bull gave up and trotted home. I gave my buddy a hug. He just looked up and gave me a dog smile.

Another time, a cow hung back and refused to follow the others. I did not realize she had just calved and was refusing to leave her baby. The new mother turned on me and charged without warning. I turned and sprinted to the fence.

Once more, Charlie got in the way of me and an angry bovine. She whirled to face him. He deftly avoided her attempts to stomp him. This gave me enough time to scoot under the fence to safety.

Dad and I later returned to the pasture with a pickup, got the new calf into its bed and slowly drove home while its mother trotted along behind us.

Charlie also helped stave off an angry pony who had dropped me with a kick. See the chapter, Snowball — Pony from Hell in this collection.

For several years, Charlie was my main playmate. He and I loved to wrestle. I would gently roll him to the ground and he would get up and ram into me, trying to knock me over. A few years later, Charlie put this play wrestling into good use.

New neighbors moved nearby to our farm when I was about 12. They rented out their pasture lot to another neighbor, who needed more grazing space for his cow herd. One day, the cattle got out and wandered up and down the gravel road.

Charlie tagged along when I went to help drive the escapees back home. The neighbor's dog, Ranger, and Charlie greeted each other with bared fangs and immediately clashed. The neighbor turned to me and said, "Your dog might get hurt, mine's part German Shepherd."

Before the words were barely out of his mouth, Charlie put his head under Ranger, flipped him upside down, pounced on top and locked his jaws on Ranger's throat.

It was a perfect "duck under" wrestling move followed by a pin. I ordered Charlie off the whimpering Ranger, who slunk back to his owner. Ranger never challenged Charlie again.

Charlie refused my order to "sic 'em" only one time. On a fall evening, while finishing chores, I heard something unusual like a loud feline growl near the barn where the chickens roosted. I ran to the back porch, grabbed our 12-gauge shotgun, a flashlight and headed for the small barn.

I shined the light up and down the fenceline that separated the cattle lot from our timber. Two luminescent green eyes shone back at me. And then came the scream. A high-pitched screech that sounded like a woman being tortured.

Charlie was standing near me, intently gazing into the trees. His hackles were raised but he made no sound. I unfastened a gate and whispered, "Go get 'em boy, sic 'em." Charlie remained statue still. I started to turn back to the house when the thing screamed again. I raised the shotgun and fired five shots where I had seen the reflection of the eyes.

I'm sure I accomplished nothing other than scaring the animal away. I backed away from the barn and headed to the house. Charlie seemed more than happy to accompany me. After telling my Dad why I fired so many shots in the dark, he smiled. "Must have been a bobcat."

Of all the things that could have brought on Charlie's downfall, it was me, his best friend. One day when in high school, I must have been late for school and was rushing to drive myself into town. I jumped in my '63 Plymouth, which was parked under a shade tree, and backed up quickly.

I forgot that Charlie liked to lie in the cool shade under vehicles. He did not move fast enough to get out. Something under the car hit him, smashing his shoulder. Charlie rolled over, got up, yelped in pain. Horrified, I watched as he looked back at me and limped away.

Charlie slowly healed, but he had a severe limp after that. My poor dog moved slower and slower after being injured.

A year and a half or so later, Charlie was trying to walk back to the barn after being fed when he fell. It was a cold March day. A thick sheet of ice coated the ground. We don't know how long he laid there valiantly trying to get up, but he couldn't manage it.

When I returned home, I rushed over to him when I saw him lying on the ground. The ice must have been partially melted when he fell, but now his side was frozen to the ground. I tried in vain to lift him, move him — anything. Nothing worked.

He continued thrashing but finally settled down when I sat down, held his head in my lap and patted him. My old friend wagged his tail and whined. I couldn't help him. With tears streaming down my cheeks, I ran into the house looking for help.

Mom and Dad shook their head and told me they tried to get him up, too, but his body was frozen solidly in the ice.

Dad looked me and said softly, "I called Doc (the veterinarian). He's on his way. There's nothing we can do for him."

I looked at Mom and Dad. "But, it's Charlie," I half sobbed, half yelled. "We've got to do something." They just shook their heads.

I was in another room when the vet arrived. It happened so fast, I could only watch helplessly from the house. Doc walked up to Charlie, knelt down and patted him while he administered the shot. Charlie wagged his tail and then he was still.

It was not the way Charlie should have died. He should have been stretched out on his favorite spot — a cool cement slab next to the house — gazing out over the farm he had protected for 13 years before succumbing to death's slumber. My friend deserved better.

~ Ben ~

After Charlie's injury, it became apparent he wouldn't be any help with the livestock. I was in high school and was responsible for the afternoon livestock chores, which included feeding the cattle and hogs.

It was always helpful to have a dog hold the critters at bay when opening and closing gates. I had been thinking of getting another dog anyway since Charlie had been slowing down over the past couple of years. Also, I would be leaving for college soon and wanted my parents to have a younger dog they could rely on.

The first puppy I brought home was a black Lab mix. However, he was only with us a month. The pup ventured too far one day and was struck by a car as he was exploring the ditch across the road.

A few weeks later, I heard about a neighbor who was giving away puppies. The litter all looked like their mother with pretty reddish-brown coats.

I watched for a while as the barely weaned pups played and nipped at each other. One of them ventured over to me, grabbed the laces on my tennis shoe and started tugging and playfully growling.

I took the little male home and named him, Ben. After thinking about it, I don't remember why the name Ben seemed right. It just did.

Charlie accepted the wiggling, friendly newcomer with more patience than I expected. The only place the older dog refused the newcomer access was his special spot — that cool cement slab by the house. Even after Charlie's death, Ben stayed away from that spot.

One irritating thing about having two sentinels — Charlie and Ben — on the farm was that I could not sneak in at odd hours of the night or early morning.

When coming home late from a date, I thought I was clever by turning off the ignition, shutting off the head lights and letting the car coast slowly into the grass just off the driveway.

But, the two dogs took their jobs seriously. They knew what my car looked and sounded like, but they barked any way. Charlie with his deep baritone and Ben with his half howl could wake up the neighborhood.

I'd roll down my window and not so kindly order them to: "Shut up, already, you stupid dogs. It's me!" Both my "fierce" watch dogs would greet me with wagging tails, wanting to be petted.

Ben's lineage also was mishmash of different breeds. He looked like a lab but was smaller. His tail curled up a bit and howled when he barked. Must have been a hound mixed in there somewhere.

The younger dog was not an alpha. He wanted to please. Ben learned quickly, a little too quickly I found out one day. While doing chores one afternoon, the hungry hogs swarmed around the gate I was trying to get through with a tractor and wagon.

I started yelling "shoo" and waving my arms. The eager Ben ran to my aid and started barking furiously. He backed up the entire herd while I drove through the gate and shut it.

After that, "shoo" became his command to chase and drive whatever I pointed at. It was not as fierce as "sic 'em!" but it worked, even with people.

Charlie would never chase or bark at a human once he made their acquaintance. Ben, however, was another story.

I found it great fun to encourage one of my nephews or other un-aware visitor to run a short distance away. I then would yell "shoo!" The mild mannered dog would streak after his target, barking, snarling and circling them. He never bit anyone. Ben quit only when I yelled "stop!" Then he would run back to me, tail wagging.

Ben only responded to my command which frustrated my nephews who would yell "shoo!" and point to me. My canine servant would just sit there and wait patiently for me to give the order.

I put Ben's herding instincts to good use when hunting squirrels in our timber. When I spotted a squirrel foraging on the ground, I'd "shoo" Ben at it. He would race after the critter, barking and circling the tree it had just scooted up.

Once squirrels think they're safe, they will scold intruders and scramble to the other side of the tree. With Ben circling and barking, the squirrel would be so intent on watching him that I always got a clear shot when it moved to watch the pesky dog.

I was away from home at the time of Ben's two most impressive accomplishments.

Mom and Dad volunteered one time to dog sit a Pekinese owned by my brother and his family when they went on vacation. This rabbit-sized canine had always lived in a house. Being a traditional farm wife, Mom did not allow animals in the house. So, he was kept just inside the barn door on a nice warm bed of straw.

Well, the Pekinese went nuts outside. He'd just run and run until he dropped. It's amazing how fast those little legs could go. One day, Mom saw him squeeze through an opening in the barn and take off for the neighbors.

Thinking she would catch up to the dumb little dog, Mom followed on foot with Ben at her side. But, the Pekinese was too far ahead and ran to the neighbor's house.

This was the same neighbor who owned the infamous Ranger years before. But now the family had two full-sized German Shepherds. The big dogs came charging around the corner of the house. The pair sniffed briefly at the Pekinese, didn't bother him but then loped toward my very nervous mother.

Mom told me later what happened. "It's a good thing that dog of yours was with me when I followed that useless Pekinese. The neighbor's dogs started running toward us. I stood still but must've said, 'Oh shoot!'"

She probably said something more colorful, but that was her version. It may make sense considering what happened next.

"Ben saved me. He charged in front of me and stood there with his hackles up and teeth bared, Mom said. "He was growling like I've never heard before! Those two German Shepherds stopped dead in their tracks looked at him and ran back off behind their house. Then I grabbed that Pekinese and got out of there."

I was proud and amazed when I heard her story. There was no way Ben could have warded off one German Shepherd, much less two of them, in a fight. I never weighed him, but he probably tipped the scales between 40 and 50 pounds.

Then something Mom said made sense to me. If she did indeed say "shoot," Ben would have heard "shoo" and obeyed her by charging at the threat. Good dog.

Ben's other "great" achievement came in the romance department. A year of so later, the same brother who had the Pekinese upgraded to a female Saint Bernard. My brother and his family lived nearby. Ben liked to visit them occasionally.

I'm not sure how he accomplished the maneuver, but Ben mated with the much larger female and produced a litter of very unusual-looking puppies. Sadly, they did not survive.

30

The mother was a rescue dog that had been mistreated. She was not in good health when the puppies were born and was unable to nurse them.

About a year later when I was home from college, I went looking for Ben but could not find him. Dad came out of the house and shook his head. "He's dead, son. Hunters shot him. They must have thought he was a fox."

Dad told me he was outside when he heard a series of shots not far from the house in our corn field. He walked out to the road and saw several hunters run out of the newly picked field, jump into pickups and drive off. Curious, Dad drove to where the hunters had been parked.

Ben lay dead at the edge of the field. He had been shot several times. My dog loved to go hunting with me. He probably saw or heard the other people and, perhaps thinking it was me, ran out to join them.

Dad told me he buried Ben underneath one of the oak trees behind the house. I walked to where he was buried. A flat piece of board was stuck in the ground to mark the spot. The words painted in black simply said:

Ben
Good dog

Ben was the last dog my parents or I would own.

3
The Nelson Place

Note: I have called this story, "The Nelson Place," in honor of my father and Roger, one of my brothers. When I visited Dad during the last few months of his life, he always asked where I was staying the night. He and Mom were in a care facility in nearby Ackley.

When I told him I was staying "at the farm," Dad would ask where it was. I'd say, "The farm southeast of Iowa Falls."

He'd look at me for a moment then say, "Oh, you're staying at the Nelson place? That's good."

At that time, Roger was living in the family farmhouse while he was looking in regularly on Mom and Dad. He started calling it "the Nelson place" to humor Dad and continued doing so after he passed away in 1993. Roger died in 2014.

The farm I grew up on was in my family for 112 years. Great-grandfather Levi Nelson (British version, sorry Scandinavians) moved his family from Illinois to the 200-acre North Central Iowa farm in 1886. My brothers and I sold it to a neighbor in 1997, a year after our mother passed away.

If you would ask any of the long-time neighbors, they still may call it "the old Williams place." My parents moved our family to the farm in 1954, when Mom's parents retired to nearby Iowa Falls. I was 2 years old. So, for the next 44 years, it was the Williams farm.

Our farmstead sat on a small rise on a north-south county gravel road. When my wife, a farm girl raised in the Mississippi River valley hills of Dubuque County, first visited the place, she wondered where was the hill I had talked about. Guess it's a matter of perception.

Even though our "hill" was a bump compared to its Eastern Iowa brethren, we still had a commanding view of the neighborhood.

Looking south, we could see the outbuildings of the farm where Dad grew up. A bit to the east of those buildings were the Elliott place, the Willems farm and the Chaplin/Diemer farm.

At night, my mother sometimes would chuckle when gazing out the south-facing living room window. "Oh look. You can see the lights of Owasa." At that time the small town, which was about six miles away across county gravel roads, consisted of a K through 6th grade school, a grain elevator and a few houses.

When I turned 10, Mom returned to teaching after staying home many years to care for me and my brothers. Her first job after returning to the profession was at Owasa, where she taught first grade.

The Walthall farm with its white buildings straight across our fields to the east always made a lovely sight at sunset. The buildings would gradually turn from an amber to burnt orange as the sun slowly sank behind our farmstead. This farm was probably less than a quarter mile "up the east road" as we used to say.

For much of my youth, all of our fields were east of the farmstead across the gravel road. The fields were rotated among oats (straw), alfalfa (hay), corn and soybeans. Our small herd of Black Angus cattle were let out daily to graze on a 30-acre pasture "just down the road."

I got to know these fields very well over the years from baling hay, walking (weeding) beans, seeding oats, picking corn, combining beans, bringing the cattle back home at night and hunting in the fall and winter.

To the north were the Brown family's acreage, the Oppold farm, Baer acreage, and a bit farther up another hill, another giant red barn stood sentinel for the Schieslaug and later Kelsey farm.

The view looking west was my favorite. A thick stand of trees heralded the beginning of our 20-acre timber. These woods were the best playground a farm boy could want whether it was exploring or hunting.

Besides every variety of bird, hawk and owl that was native to Central Iowa, a wide variety of other wild creatures lived or passed through "the timber." (See the Menagerie story in this collection.)

The most pervasive pest to inhabit the timber, though, was the mosquito. During summers at dusk, you could hear the high-pitched hum of perhaps billions of those bloodsuckers from the driveway entrance, which was easily two football fields or more away. The mosquitoes made trips to the timber during the summer a miserable experience.

Our farmstead had an assortment of buildings ranging from our two-story wood-frame house, two barns, two steel grain bins, two corn cribs, two garages (one for a car and the other for a pickup and/or tractor), a large lean-to style machine shed, a pump house, a workshop that looked like a small house and various other outbuildings that one time or another housed chickens, hogs, corncobs and junk accumulated over 100 years.

This was the perfect setting for a young boy who liked to disappear for hours with a book or to just hide out. If company showed up unannounced with people I did not want to associate with, I could escape to one of those buildings. Much to my delight, no one could FInd me even if they looked.

When the company departed, my mother would get her feral child's attention by calling: "They're gone. Come on out wherever you are. For heaven's sake come in for supper!" Being a school teacher, my mother possessed a distinctive voice. Only a bit taller than 5 feet, she could project her voice to be heard anywhere around the farm.

The first thing anyone saw when driving towards our place was a classic Iowa red barn just off the road right before turning into the driveway. My grandfather built the "big barn" to store hay and straw and house cattle. The front had two open doors where cattle could gather to escape the elements if need be.

A door near the peak of the roof could be opened during haying season. One of the hay crew, usually Dad, would stab a multi-pronged rope fork into a stack of bales. The stack would be lifted through the door via a pulley and dropped into the hay mow. The space for the mow in the center of the barn was huge. When full, it could hold almost a story and half full of hay.

After the hay was "put up," my friends and I loved to make forts out of the bales. Sometimes these fortresses would be three or four bales high and four or five across. We would have complained if we would have been told to stack them that way, but it was different because it was our idea.

Two smaller mows were above the cattle-loafing areas. You had to be careful when walking across those areas. Both of the small mow floors had square holes cut into them to allow bales to be dropped for the cattle below.

An OSHA inspector of the future may have had a heart attack if he/she would have seen a skinny teenager dragging bales across the floor, use a large pocketknife to cut off the twine and shove sections through the hole to waiting cattle. Boards sometimes were placed over the openings but not always. The rule was if you were old enough to be in that area, you'd better remember where those holes were located.

Animal-rights sympathizers also might have had an issue with my hay-distribution method. It was great fun to drop a chunk of the bale onto the head of an ornery cow. The critter was never hurt. She would just shake off the pieces and continue munching.

As with all barns of this area, it sported a cupola in the middle of the peak. These unique structures, which sometimes resemble castle turrets, serve as a vent, especially important after new hay is cut and harvested.

Much to Dad's chagrin, our cupola also was the perfect nesting and roosting spot for pigeons. I had standing permission to shoot the pesky birds.

Swallows also made their mud nests in the rafters of the big barn. They would dart in and out of the open doors chattering in their unique way. Those little birds also loved it when I mowed the grass. They would swoop over, in front and to the side of me like dive bombers snagging juicy insects that were trying to escape the onslaught of my riding mower.

The small barn was closer to the house and about half as tall but was wider. It actually was the original barn and was built to be a multi-purpose structure.

One third of the space had been the milking area. The cows would saunter in and poke their heads through the wooden stanchions to get to the feed bunk on the other side. The milking crew would lock the stanchions to keep the animals from moving around during milking.

Dad sold the dairy cows when my three older brothers graduated high school and left to make their way in the world. Being the youngest of four boys by quite a few years, I never got to experience the "pleasure" of milking cows by hand. I've always been grateful for that.

This barn was a wonderful place to play hide-and-seek. It had at least four doorways to the outside. Besides the milking/feeding area, the interior included four small pens, usually reserved for cows or sows ready to give birth.

The loft was smaller than its counterpart in the big barn. We usually "put up" straw or grass hay in this space. At the time, most of the straw in our area came after oats were harvested. The oat straw (basically the stems) were left to dry, then baled and used for bedding.

Baling and putting up straw was a dusty and dirty chore. More than once I was rendered useless due to sneezing and coughing fits. Whereas alfalfa hay was wet, green and heavy, straw was lighter but the dust and the stems covered your body and stuck everywhere. My arms often were covered with scratches after handling the straw bales.

A wall extended across the width the mow. Inside the loft, sacks of feed and equipment were stored in a small room. A small granary was in the next room, but access to this space was on the outside.

The roof of these rooms made an excellent platform or deck. More straw or supplies could be stored here. This area offered another quiet hide-out for a certain farm boy.

All these nooks and crannies, filled with hay or straw also made perfect places for the farm cats to curl up in warm bedding during winter or find hiding places to birth their kittens. Heat from the bodies of the cattle or hogs helped warm the building.

Feeder cattle or hogs were housed on the opposite side of the barn from the milking area. One of the many doors let the animals have access to yet another lot. A decent-sized storage area was located on the other side of the inside wall.

Dad bought a used fuel truck and stored it there. He said he had plans for that truck, but it never left its "temporary" garage. The vehicle did make for a fun plaything for myself and for grandchildren later on.

Almost twenty years have passed since my brothers and I sold the crop ground and later on, the farmstead. High winds or possible tornadoes have brought down both barns. The farmstead has changed hands several times, and the new owners have added their touches and no doubt much-needed improvements.

To paraphrase the late-Kurt Vonnegut Jr. — one of my favorite authors — my home still exists as it was. It exists in my memory. I don't need to visit to look at it. I can see it clearly in my mind.

4
Tough First Day

I'm sure many people remember their first day of school. Yours truly is no exception. My first day of school also included a valuable vocabulary lesson.

Most of Sept. 3, 1957, is a blank. Partly due to the retention capacity of my childish brain and partly because of the abject terror of being placed in the middle of about twenty swarming, strange kindergarteners.

I had celebrated my fifth birthday two days earlier. Mom, a former school teacher, thought her youngest fledgling needed socialization with kids my age. I didn't have much contact with younger kids. My brothers were much older than me. One was in college, another was getting ready to go into the Army, the third was a junior in high school.

The socialization experiment began a week before when Mom dropped me off at Sunday school for the first time. It did not go well.

I believe I spent the majority of the hour under a desk while my fellow Methodist-trainees tried to entice me with offers of puzzles and games to come out. They should have offered me chocolate-chip cookies. I'm pretty sure I would have come out for that.

With that incident under my belt, I was presented with the next culture shock — public school. I remember some kid crying and clinging to his mother's leg thinking he was being abandoned. Oh yeah, that was me. Hopefully, I settled down for the next couple of hours. The school day for kindergarteners at that time was only from 9 a.m. to noon.

I'm sure my parents tried to prepare me for what I was supposed to do after school. Actually, it was pretty simple. Board a school bus and be driven home with the other farm kids.

I remember the end of my first day very clearly. It's amazing how traumatic events get burned into your brain. Probably 15 minutes or so before dismissal, my teacher asked: "Whoever lives in a rural area, please raise your hand."

About half a dozen hands shot up. I looked around, puzzled. What was this "rural area" she was talking about? Hmm, those were new words to my ears.

In my defense, I had never heard the word, rural, before. Yes, our address was Rural Route 2, but most letters came addressed with RR 2 on them.

All of my relatives and friends knew my family lived on a farm. We never said when asked by a stranger where we lived: "Why, yes, we live in a rural area about six miles south of town.

So, my classmates and I followed our teacher outside. Some kids climbed into cars lined up outside the school. A few others, who lived close by, started walking home with their parents and a handful of other children, those who raised their hands after the teacher asked that curious question, got into a yellow station wagon with a sign attached to the roof that said "SCHOOL BUS."

Guess who couldn't read at the time? Me. I knew what a school bus looked like. It was a large, box-like yellow monster that my brothers rode daily.

I stood there patiently and waited for a school bus to come and watched the exodus of the other kids. After a few minutes, my teacher came over and stood with me. All the other vehicles and bodies eventually disappeared and there we stood.

She finally said: "Aren't your parents coming to get you?"

I looked up and helpfully replied: "Oh no I'm supposed to get on the school bus."

She looked at bit concerned and then asked, "Where do you live?"

Now this was one question I could answer. "I live on a farm in the country."

I don't recall her expression, but she took my hand and led me back into school. We stopped at the office where she talked briefly to the school secretary. The other lady started to search through some records when she stopped and looked at me. "Dear, would you happen to know your phone number?"

Nodding cheerfully, I correctly repeated the number, which Mom had been drilling me to remember for the past several months. The secretary called home, chatted for a minute and hung up. "Your mother will be here in a half hour."

My teacher nodded and took me to the cafeteria. I was given a tray, silverware, watched the lunch ladies plop the specialty of the day on my tray and give me a strange little carton that had milk it — imagine that.

We sat down at one of the long tables where I nibbled at the strange food and looked around in wonderment at the commotion of the older students chatting, wolfing down their lunches and running out to recess. When I finished, my teacher guided me back to the office where I waited for my chauffeur.

My Mom was a bit embarrassed at the trouble I had stirred up and apologized for any inconvenience I had caused. The secretary said it was not a problem and this wasn't the first time they had to take care of a confused rookie.

Mom looked at me and asked, "Why didn't you get on the school bus?" The secretary helpfully related what had happened, and they both started laughing. We didn't leave the school until everyone was reassured I knew I was supposed to ride the "mini bus," which I did dutifully after that.

The next year, during the first day of first grade, my teacher asked, "Does anyone know how to go through the cafeteria?" No longer a rookie, I raised my hand. The teacher smiled and nodded. "Oh yes, Myron, I know you have been there before."

I now realize that my not-so-successful first day of kindergarten was probably "the story of the day" among the teachers in their lounge, where they escaped to regain some semblance of their sanity.

The first-grade teacher let me guide my classmates through that industrial feeding system we all would become familiar with for the next 12 years. I had to show some of them where to find the milk. Rookies — sheesh.

Vignette I. Bumps, Bangs & Bruises

I was fortunate not to have been injured very seriously while working and playing around the farm. There were close calls like falling out of a hay mow and landing squarely on my butt.

I also stepped on a nail or two, whacked my head or scraped most areas of body on something or other. Quite a few times, I threw my back out after carrying heavy buckets of feed.

My pony did her best to knock me for a loop several times, too. See Snowball – Pony from Hell in this collection. I only escaped from an angry bull after my dog rushed in and deflected his attention.

I now wince at all the near misses or dangerous situations I have could have gotten into. A friend and neighbor, Myrln Bartling Sr., was killed when he became entangled in a power-takeoff.

During my ag journalism career, I got to work with several farm safety specialists and learned of the horror stories about many serious injuries and sad fatalities that have occurred to all ages of people on farms.

I never second guessed riding in the tractor bucket when it was raised eight to ten feet off the ground when Dad was driving or riding on the tractor's hitch or next to Dad's seat while it bounced along in a bumpy field.

Unfortunately, a couple of my relatives didn't fare as well. My brother, Roger, got stung severely when he dug into a bumble-bee nest while shelling corn. My parents put my brother, who was going into shock, in the back seat of our car, grabbed me and raced to the hospital six miles away in Iowa Falls.

I remember watching in terror as the nurses threw blankets on him to try to stop his uncontrolled shivering while the doctors gave him shots to counteract the poison in his system. Roger recovered but he had to wear a medical-alert bracelet the rest of his life.

This was nothing like the wasp stings I got at age 3 when Mom pushed me outside to play on the back porch. I was told I threw a fit and was jumping up and down on the old wooden platform which upset the wasps and led to multiple stings.

My Grandpa Nelson had his ribs broken by a bull when it kept head butting him against a fence. The only thing that saved him was the flexibility of the wire. He probably would have been crushed if it had been a wooden fence.

Mom said poor Grandpa kept bouncing off the wire while the bull tried to gore him. The beast finally got bored with the game and allowed Grandpa to stumble out of the pen. The animal was carted off to market the next day.

5
Fun with Big Wheels

One thing about growing up on a farm is most kids get to play with really big toys at a young age. Tractors and other machinery are definitely not toys, but try telling that to a 10-year-old boy driving a massive machine through a hayfield or on a rural road.

Dad usually owned three tractors — all Cases. Two were 1940s smallish chore machines, which I was allowed to drive. The other was a late 1960s field tractor, a larger, newer machine that sported the new Case yellow look.

Dad liked this particular orange and yellow brand for some reason. This was well before the Case-IH merger that turned all their tractors and other farm machinery IH red.

He told me the IH tractors were "pretty good" but did not like those dark green ones — John Deere. Dad laughed and called them Johnny Putt-Putts. True enough, one of our neighbors drove an older Deere, and you could hear the classic pop, pop, pop of the exhaust as it chugged through his fields.

Come to think of it, I believe each our neighbors drove a different brand and color of tractor. Milo W. to the east had a little silver Ford. Just north of us was the Deere guy. Other neighbors had Farmalls, Masseys, IH's and the other green brand — Oliver. Yes, we were a truly integrated neighborhood — tractor-wise anyway.

My first adventure or misadventure, rather, driving a tractor was at age 8 when I was trying to steer one of our older ones. Dad and I were rounding up some of our cattle that decided to go sightseeing at the neighbor's acreage. I went along to "help."

Dad's instructions were quick and to the point. "Push in the stick (clutch) to make it go, pull back on a handle near the seat to give it gas and step on the brakes to stop."

Dad, who would quickly learn he had a mechanically challenged son, forgot to mention a vital piece of information — pull back on the clutch to stop the engine. Uh-oh.

Everything went fine — for awhile. I did just fine rolling along in second gear, steering the strays back through a hole in the fence. Then, one calf brook loose and made a break for greener pastures. I pursued the critter and it headed for the only tree in sight.

I circled the tree and got the calf to head back to the herd. But, somehow I had turned the tractor so sharply I could not pull it out of the turn. The tractor slowly circled and got closer and closer to the tree.

I stood on the brakes, but the tractor kept going, though it chugged and lurched a bit. Dad was standing at the hole in the fence to keep the cattle from running back through. He turned around with a shocked look and yelled, "Pull the clutch, pull the clutch."

Those directions could have been in a foreign language to a now-frightened 8-year-old. I was frantically stomping on the brakes, when my brain finally translated what Dad was yelling — "oh, pull the stick." I yanked the stick back and the tractor stopped within a few feet of colliding with the tree.

A muttering Dad finally made his way over and relieved me of my driving duties. I wasn't allowed on a tractor again until I reached the ripe old age of 10, when I was a bit bigger and stronger and then it was for chores that required the snail's pace in second gear.

Another couple years later, I earned back Dad's confidence in my tractor-driving skills to the extent he let me take it on the road, though only to reach one of our fields usually only a tenth of a mile or so away.

I became the tractor errand boy. This usually entailed fetching a full grain wagon or hay rack and towing them back the farmstead or running back home to grab a tool needed to fix a break-down. This was great fun and I didn't shirk my responsibilities too badly as described in the Where'd that Boy Go? story in this collection.

One time, I had the brilliant idea of taking one of the chore tractors to bring the cow herd back from the day pasture. Now this may have worked great if all those bovines behaved.

I drove the short distance, opened the gate as usual and waited for the thirsty creatures to amble back home to get a drink of water. Well, the noise of the tractor spooked some of the calves. They turned and ran back into the pasture.

"No problem," I thought. Most of the herd headed toward home as usual. I drove the tractor into the pasture to round up the runaways, but the youngsters quickly learned they could outmaneuver the clumsy machine and scattered even more.

Even my dog, Charlie, looked up at me as if he was saying: "Which one should I chase?" I sat there stewing for a moment, shut off the tractor, and Charlie and I rounded up the stragglers on foot. A half-hour later, I drove the tractor back home with Charlie faithfully following me.

Mom, who had been posted as usual to be the lookout for oncoming cars did not appreciate what usually was a 15-minute job that turned into almost an hour. She let me know in no uncertain terms about her displeasure.

Another idea that sounded good also blew up in practice.

My one attempt to do serious fieldwork did not go well. For some reason, Dad thought it was a good idea for me to try my hand at planting beans with the big tractor.

I was excited for the opportunity see what all the fuss was about to drive up and down the rows of a field. This time Dad actually explained things pretty well.

"Drive to the end of the row, slow down, pull up the marker arm (a straight metal 8-foot or so pole with a knife-like piece at the end that cut through the tilled soil), turn the tractor and planter around and follow the trail back to the other end and repeat."

OK, got it. I did just fine and managed a few rounds until I came to the end of the row where a wagon was parked. I misjudged the distance between the wagon and marker arm. As I made my turn and pulled up the arm, it caught the side of the wagon and bent back.

Dad was pretty upset and let me know about it — loudly. He spent the next few hours pounding the marker back into shape, and I spent that time being as far away as possible. So much for becoming a field hand.

The most fun I had driving a tractor was during hay season. If I was not picked to be on the hay rack lifting and stacking bales in the field, I got to operate the tractor that controlled the hay fork.

Thinking back on it, the Rube Goldberg procedure was a pretty interesting feat of engineering. I will try to relate all the steps correctly.

A hay fork that looked like a giant clamp with large hooks for teeth was used to grab onto a stack of bales. A large rope that was connected to the fork was tied to the tractor. The rope also was fastened to a pulley that led into a large open door just under the peak of the roof.

When a hay rack piled high with small square bales was being unloaded, the tines of the fork were stabbed into the bales. After making sure the fork was clamped and locked in place, the rack man (usually Dad) would shout to the tractor driver. I would slowly back the tractor up, which lifted the stack up to the pulley.

The stack rose into the air, clicked into place on the pulley and zoomed down a metal track into the barn. A helper inside the barn (worst job ever) would yell when the stack reached the spot he wanted it dumped.

Dad would shout — whoa! — for me to stop, then yank on another rope that released the fork. The second shout — OK! — was my signal to put the tractor in gear and race down a small incline toward the barn which lowered the fork to be refastened onto a fresh stack of bales and the procedure would be repeated.

It was easy duty being the rope driver. You backed up until told to stop. Then got to drive as fast as the tractor could go before slamming on the brakes and hopefully not hitting anyone or anything on the way back.

As I got into my mid and later teens, I got to pull wagonloads of grain and full hay racks back to the farm. I quickly learned to use a lower gear after the tractor start chugging and lurching.

It sometimes was a "white-knuckle" ride pulling a hay rack stacked eight rows high up an incline on our gravel road. The tractor groaned under the pressure, and the load of hay would rock back and forth, causing the rack to wobble from side to side.

All that and trying to keep the tractor and rack on the right side of the road and out of the ditch made for an interesting trip home.

Vignette II. Birds and the Bees

Farm kids learn early on about the birds and the bees. It's a fact of life. To use a popular phrase from a Disney movie — "it's the circle of life." It is common to see the entire process — from mating to birth to maturing to market — in a span of a season (hogs and other smaller livestock species) to a little over a year with cattle.

As with a lot of common knowledge, I may have been a little slow to the party — again. (See Tough First Day in this collection.) I was probably 8 or 9 when I got my first biology lesson.

A few years earlier, Mom and Dad thought it would be fun to raise ducks. Unlike chickens, which didn't venture too far from the farm buildings, the ducks wandered everywhere — around the house, the garden and the yard. It was common to look out any window to see the pair of domesticated Mallards (and later Muscovies) waddling by looking for bugs or nesting sites.

One morning while having breakfast in our summer kitchen, I watched in horror as the drake chased down and mounted the hen. Before Dad could stop me, I rushed outside and "rescued" the hen from her attacker. Both ducks quacked their displeasure at the rude interruption and shuffled off to find a more peaceful place for their interlude.

Proud of my chivalrous actions, I returned to the table and announced I had saved the hen, yet again. Dad cast a slightly amused look at me. Mom chuckled. "The male's not hurting her. They are mating. That's what they do so they can lay eggs and have babies," he explained.

As I'm writing this, I realize Dad was giving me "the talk" but putting it in livestock terms. He then proceeded to tell me it was the same thing as breeding with the bigger animals. I had heard those words before but all of a sudden the light bulb went off as to what they meant.

I took a few more bites of my cereal and stopped as a thought occurred to me. "I guess I shouldn't chase the ducks when they do that or the roosters when they jump on the hens?" I now had both parents' attention.

Mom walked over, smiling and asked, "How long have you been doing this?" I told her for most of the spring when I caught the perpetrators. Dad just shook his head.

I thought some more. "So, that's what the bull is doing to the cows and the boar to the sows, huh?"

"That's right," Dad said. I think he was relieved he had gotten the first phase of the talk out of the way so casually.

"Guess I'll stop throwing rocks at them then," I said with a shrug and returned to my Frosted Flakes.

Dad started choking and managed to sputter, "You've been doing what?"

I looked up. "I thought the bull and the boars were hurting the females so I've been throwing rocks at them until they stopped." Mom burst out in an explosion of laughter and walked out of the room.

Dad — not usually at a loss for words — just sat there with an incredulous look on his face. He finally managed to say, "No, don't ever do that again. You might hurt them besides we need them to do that so they will have babies."

I promised I would stop separating the copulating couples with my missiles and returned to my cereal. Dad got up and went outside, muttering to himself. I could still hear Mom laughing somewhere in the house.

6
Menagerie

When I was growing up, our farm was home to an interesting zoo-like mix of domestic and wild creatures. Of course, we had the usual domestic livestock — cows, hogs and chickens as well as cats and dogs.

Our chickens were free range well before this term was coined. The birds were mostly left to their own resources. They had run of the entire farmstead. Their diets consisted of the insects they could catch as well as spilled grain around the hog feeders and cattle troughs.

The hens nested wherever they could find a place to squeeze in among the hay or straw bales in the small barn. At night, the chickens would flap up and roost on a crossbeam that ran the width of the old milking area. The birds were safe when a dog was present to scare off the varmints.

Nighttime offered the best chance to "harvest" birds that were destined for the dinner table.

Dad had a long piece of wire with a hook at the end of it. He'd wait until dark, grab a flashlight and his leg-grabbing wire then quietly walk under the roosting beam.

After spotting his chicken of choice, he'd hook the wire on its legs and give a yank. The doomed bird only had time for a quick squawk before it was stuffed into a bag where it would be quickly dispatched. Unable to see, the other birds remained quiet on the beam.

Mom usually would greet me in the morning by saying something like: "I heard a couple of hens squawking earlier. Go look for those fresh eggs when you get a chance."

The hens had their favorite spots to lay eggs. If I was lucky, I would find a couple of eggs that recently were laid without the hen present.

However, many times the egg distributor would be in its nest. If I was lucky, the hen would squawk angrily at me and flutter away.

It was not a good sign if the hen was quiet and refused to move. This meant she was in her "setting" or nesting mode to incubate the eggs until they hatched.

Of course, I always forgot to wear gloves. So, I would try to slowly inch my exposed hand and arm under the protective mother in an effort to steal one of her precious eggs.

Again, if I was lucky, I'd get away with a warning peck. However, if the hen possessed the feisty Bantam genetics, I'd come away looking like I lost a fight with a cheese grater.

(A more detailed description of my egg-hunting adventures can be found in the Chore Boy chapter.)

Our poultry flock flourished despite being left to its own resources. We usually kept three or four roosters with eight or nine hens. This was enough to give us fresh eggs regularly as well as provide the entrees for those traditional Sunday dinners.

The chickens were an interesting mishmash of breeds that probably were introduced by my grandparents or great-grandparents. Mom liked to gaze at the flock and guess their heritage.

"See that that rooster with the red feathers? He must be a Rhode Island Red. That white hen over there must have some Leghorn in her. Those small, black and white hens are definitely Banties (Bantams)."

Each member in a new brood of chicks usually wound up looking nothing like its siblings. During the summer, the dutiful mothers could be heard clucking to their youngsters.

The hens usually raised enough chicks to keep our family in meat and eggs and continue the flock for another year.

Ducks were added later on and brought their own goofy flair to the atmosphere. A neighbor raised waterfowl and gave us some fertilized eggs.

Since we didn't have a mother duck, the neighbor suggested the next best thing — a setting hen. So, Dad removed the chicken eggs and carefully replaced them with the larger duck eggs. Then we waited, a bit dubiously.

It takes about three weeks for chicks to hatch after incubation starts. The neighbor told us it takes four weeks for ducklings to break out of their shells. He joked it took an extra week for the webbed feet and bigger beaks to develop.

We wondered if the mother hen would stay on the nest for that extra week. Hens eventually will abandon a nest if their eggs don't hatch.

Four weeks was a lot to ask a bird that was wired to expect babies after 21 days.

I was maybe 8 or 9 when we tried the duck experiment. Every few days, I would peek at the mother hen, which was protected nicely among some straw bales in the barn.

After several weeks, I lost track of time and my visits grew fewer and fewer as the incubation dragged on.

One day, I heard some strange peeping noises coming from the barn. Curious, I looked in on the hen. To my amazement, three or four ducklings peeked out from under the feathers of their foster mother.

The hen clucked and dutifully attended to her new offspring. She didn't seem upset by their odd little bills or strange noises. A day later, the hen emerged from her nest, trailed by six ducklings who followed her everywhere.

Even though they were different species, the ducklings learned her different clucks: "follow me," "I found food" or "danger."

It was amusing to see the ducklings trail after the hen. When she avoided a sizable mud puddle, her strange offspring would dive right in and swim through the water.

Only two of the six ducklings grew to adulthood — a drake and a hen. The pair bonded and mated but never produced any babies, probably because they were siblings.

This first pair looked like wild Mallards. The male sported a dark green head, dark-brown breast and multi-colored plumage. The hen was a speckled brown. They were larger than their wild cousins and could not fly.

About a year later, Dad visited the neighbor with the ducks and brought back a clutch of eggs of a different breed — Muscovy.

Dad found the Mallard pair's nest and replaced their eggs with the new ones. He also placed a few eggs under a setting hen.

Our female Mallard never knew the difference and hatched her first and only brood. The chicken also successfully hatched her brood of ducklings. All of a sudden, we had ducks everywhere.

The Muscovy is an odd-looking bird. It looks like a turkey vulture with webbed, clawed feet. This breed, which originates from Central America and is not related to Mallards, has a turkey like "comb," which stretches from its bill to cover about half its face. The drake combs are larger than what the hens have.

Muscovies come in all colors from all white and black to everything in between. We learned other interesting characteristics about this breed — they rarely quack and can fly.

After the first batch of our Muscovy ducklings matured, they started taking aerial explorations of the farm. It became normal to see our small flock circle the farmstead several times.

They always came back. Once they grew larger, their flying became limited to a few hundred feet barely above the ground.

Our Mallard drake turned into Casanova the next spring when the Muscovy hens reached breeding age. Several of the new broods of ducklings were Muscovy-Mallard crossbreds.

That fall, we had Mallards and young Muscovies circling the farm on their patrol flights.

Once the Muscovy drakes grew larger, they also became aggressive. The males emitted a hiss when upset or fighting for a hen. Our poor Mallard drake soon became a second-class citizen to his much larger counterparts.

After butchering and cooking a few of the young Muscovies, we discovered they had a gamey flavor. But, the cross between the two breeds proved to be quite tasty.

So, we harvested the young Muscovy drakes early, and once more our little Mallard drake became sultan of a respectable harem for another year or two.

During the height of the Muscovy population explosion, I found a newly hatched duckling wandering alone, chirping forlornly. I picked up the yellow ball of fluff and brought it into the house.

For the next few days, we kept the little critter in a large cardboard grocery box and fed it oatmeal, which he eagerly gobbled up.

One time, when I was walking by the box, I heard a chirp and then a click. I turned around and saw the duckling perched on the corner of the box.

He had jumped almost twice his height to get out. After that impressive feat, I named him Hercules.

We let our little super hero waddle around for another day or two until Mom had had enough of cleaning up his "deposits." I reluctantly took Hercules outside and found a Muscovy hen leading a new batch of ducklings.

Not knowing what would happen, I put the orphan down and he promptly joined the brood. Even though the Muscovy drakes are aggressive, the hens are very good mothers. The female inspected Hercules for a moment and accepted him as one of her own.

I easily could have lost track of my former pet as he grew bigger. However, one young duck would run over to me whenever I was outside.

He'd chirp at me once or twice, peck at my shoes, pull my shoe-strings and return to the flock. Hercules' visits dwindled as he matured, but he remained much tamer than the other ducks.

Besides the domestic animals, our farm was a popular stopover, way station or crossroads for all sorts of wild creatures. It was common to see groundhogs, badgers, red foxes, pheasants, jack rabbits and cottontail rabbits going about their business in our fields across the gravel road from the farmstead.

The twenty acres of timber, just to the west of our buildings, was home to raccoons, opossums, white-tail deer, at least one bobcat, skunks, red squirrels and numerous other rodents.

Several species of hawks and owls also hunted from the sky and nearby trees. Bats and night hawks swooped around in the early evening, scooping up insects.

The songs, chirps and calls from dozens of birds could be heard from dawn until dusk: robins, blue jays, cardinals, sparrows, wrens, red-headed woodpeckers, flickers, thrushes, orioles, nut hatches, gold finches, red-wing blackbirds, starlings and boisterous crows.

Barn swallows nested on the beams in the large barn by the road. These little birds loved to dive bomb me when I mowing, snatching bugs out of the air or swooping just in front of the mower to grab insects trying to escape the onslaught of the riding mower.

Pigeons also lived in the cupola of the big barn and swooped through the farmyard looking for spilled grain.

In the fall, the two-acre pond in our cattle pasture attracted a wide variety of migrating ducks and geese. More than once, I crept through the corn stalks and bagged Sunday dinner.

Yes, we had ducks and chickens within easy reach around the farmstead, but there was something exciting and fulfilling about completing a successful hunt.

The most unusual "pet" I was given arrived by way of a thunderstorm. After heavy winds had subsided after a rainy summer night, one of our neighbors found a young sparrow hawk (kestrel) huddled on the ground. The fledgling must have been blown out of its nest.

Thinking I would enjoy taking care of the bird, neighbor Milo W gathered it up and gave it to us. Sparrow hawks are not much bigger than a robin.

Even though small, the new addition to our menagerie was not to be tamed. Someone took a picture of me, perhaps at age 8 or 9, holding my arm out as far as I could and covering my face as the little hawk flapped on my gloved hand. Guess I wasn't destined to practice falconry.

We kept it in a large cage and fed it raw hamburger. After a few days, it was obvious the little raptor wanted out and looked to be ready to fly. We released it, and it fluttered onto a branch of a large oak tree near the house.

For about another week, we would put a piece of meat on a wooden fence post. Dad set out some mouse traps. Every other meal, we'd substitute a dead rodent with raw hamburger.

The sparrow hawk would let out a shrill shriek, swoop down, "capture" the meat and enjoy the meal. It then would return to its perch in the tree.

One day, it didn't swoop down. The hawk had flown away. We had done our job.

Later that summer while I was messing around in the yard, something swooped over my head and shrieked. Of course I ducked, then looked up to see a sparrow hawk circle the yard. It shrieked again, did one more flyover and flew back into the timber.

I guess that was our hawk's way of either saying goodbye or complain that we didn't have an easy meal waiting on the fencepost.

7
Where'd That Boy Go?

It's an understatement to say I was a reluctant "gopher" (errand runner) on our farm. A lot of farm boys grow up shadowing their fathers and soak up everything they did and said. Unfortunately for Dad, I wasn't one those tag-a-longs.

Given a choice, I would have rather been playing ball with the neighborhood kids, watching old movies or reading. Yep, a geek. That label meant something entirely different in the 1960s-70s. I believe the term back in the day was "bookworm."

Like most farm kids, I was called on to help with repairs and maintenance with everything from machinery to other assorted tasks. I'd help when asked. Grasp a wrench here while Dad tightened something there or hold a flashlight (usually in the wrong spot because I couldn't see what the heck he was working on.)

I also was sent on errands to find a tool, screwdriver, socket set, grease gun, nuts and bolts, nails (different sizes were stowed in dozens of coffee tins), hammers, saws, twine — you name it.

In fairness to me, Dad had his own way of organizing his collection of tools and parts. In fairness to him, I really didn't pay too much attention to his system. Those two facts made for an awkward working relationship.

My truancy started rather innocently. Many of you may be familiar with the "Family Circle" comic strip. When one of the characters — Billy — is sent on an errand, his route winds up looking like a pirate's zig-zagging treasure map. Right turn at the sandbox, climb a tree, run over to pet the dog, play catch with the neighbor kids. You get it — he wanders all over.

Billy had nothing on me. If I was sent to the shop to fetch a seven-eighths wrench, I'd pet a cat or two on the way there, stop to get a drink of water, stare at the dried raccoon pelt hanging from the rafters and wonder how old that thing was, then try to find the wrench.

Of course my train of thought had long left the station and was headed down the wrong track. I'd think: Hmm, now what size did he want? Five-eighths? Seven-sixteenths? Yeah, that sounded right.

In the spirit of inefficiency, I'd take him both wrong sizes and offer them to him hoping one would work. Now, Dad was not the most-patient man but he'd glance at the wrenches, sigh and repeat his original request: "I said a seven-eighths wrench. It's right on the wall, right in front of your nose."

Well, that didn't help because the last thing I remember my nose pointing at was the hairless raccoon pelt which now sported only a very sad-looking tail and a remnant of a nose. So, I'd trudge back to the workshop and look a little harder. If lucky, I'd actually find that seven-eighths wrench, which meant I probably had to hold the thing while he twisted something off or tightened some other thing. By now, you should be able to detect my inattention to detail.

As I got older, I became better at finding stuff but became more irritating to work with. Usually in the middle of whatever project, I'd start to say those words that every parent hates: "Are we done yet?" My variation of: "Are we there yet?"

Don't worry, my children paid me back and then some in their early years for my juvenile behavior.

Dad usually didn't release me from my bondage until the job was done. However, if he needed a different tool and sent me on a mission to find it, good luck seeing me for awhile. This didn't help our working relationship and certainly didn't speed up the job at hand.

Also as I got older, I learned how to disappear — very quickly. If I was sitting in the house and saw Dad drive in with the pickup, I'd bolt out a door on the opposite side and melt into the timber or take shelter in of our many outbuildings. Our old farmhouse had doors on almost all sides. If someone came in the "east door" or "north door," I'd escape out the "south door."

My actions often inspired my exasperated father to loudly voice his displeasure. "Now, where'd that boy go?" I did learn, though, not to push his patience meter. Usually, he'd sigh and go off and try to do whatever task he had in store for me by himself or wait until his escaped offspring returned. I always came back for meals.

However, if he started calling for me, I'd wait to see if the volume and vocabulary increased a notch. If his yell got more colorful and/or louder, I'd reappear and act as if I had been doing something important. Like that task he asked me to do the week before.

I'm not sure my poor father ever figured out my escape routes or techniques. But, every now and then he'd walk in quietly from the south door and catch me watching TV or reading. That was unfair. Who in the heck ever comes in the from the south door anyway?

8
Snowball — Pony From Hell

I woke up on my 12th birthday with a feeling something was different. It was a warm September day. The combination window in my bedroom, which was on the second floor of our old, wood-frame farmhouse, was open a crack.

The animals were making their usual noises — robins were singing, bluejays were sounding their alarms and sparrows were chirping — but a new sound permeated my consciousness. Munch, munch, munch.

I arose and squinted out the window. Something small and white slowly moved around in the front yard. I couldn't see too clearly without the new pair of glasses I had just gotten a week or so earlier.

The white blob looked like a sheep, which would have been a strange sight since we didn't raise sheep. We had everything else — a small herd of black Angus cattle, hogs, chickens and even ducks.

Curious, I raced downstairs, grabbed my glasses and bolted out the door to take a closer look at the creature. It was very unusual for any animal to be in the fenced front yard. My mother was very protective of her Asian lilies, hollyhocks and peonies. No animal other there than our intrepid watch dog, Charlie, was allowed there.

Still in my pajamas, I raced around the lily bed and came face to muzzle with a pony. The white filly paid no attention attention to me as she chowed down on the long grass, which yours truly was supposed to mow that day.

Recalling the scene, I must have looked a bit like the character, Ralphie, in the movie, A Christmas Story. A pony! Wow, a pony! I had been asking for a pony for years. I jumped when something bumped my leg.

Charlie wanted attention. I reached down and patted his head. Our morning ritual over, he eyed the newcomer that was grazing peacefully and looked at me as if asking, "Want me to chase that thing away?" I assured him it was OK so he laid down in the grass by my feet. In retrospect, I should have let him chase that thing away.

I was still admiring my new steed when Mom and Dad interrupted my reverie by calling out, "Happy birthday!" They were sitting on the front steps watching their "wannabe" cowboy. Dad was smiling, but Mom looked dubious. I ran over and yelled, "You got me a pony! Thanks!"

Dad got up and walked over the small creature. The filly's back was about even to my shoulders. I was a small, skinny kid. So, the two of us made a less-than-imposing sight together.

"She's not broke yet and is too young to be ridden until next spring, but you can start training her to lead," Dad told me. He continued with the words that should have been a warning instead of just casual information. "Oh, she was raised with other livestock and learned to kick to protect herself when she's feeding."

Probably most of what he said was lost on me. I already was imagining riding around the countryside, waving at the neighbors as we galloped by. I could almost hear them saying, "Well, there goes that Williams boy. Whew, I've never seen a pony move that fast."

When I came back to reality, Dad was still talking. "She'll need to be fed, brushed, hooves trimmed and the manure cleaned out of her pen in the winter." I nodded in agreement but was not overjoyed at having even more manure to scoop. Now that I had reached the age and size to be a decent chore boy, manure shoveling had become one of my new responsibilities.

"Uh huh, OK," I said. Then, I got to the important question. "Who's going to break her?"

Dad looked at me, half smiled and said words which were never going to come true. "You are."

I looked at him, waiting for him to laugh at his own joke and tell me who was going to train this critter. He wasn't joking. My Dad grew up with horses. As a teenager, he raced his family's horses at the county fair and won his fair share of contests. At least that's what he claimed.

As a Williams boy, it was assumed horsemanship was in my blood. My three older brothers were good riders. Some of my first memories were of them whooping and hollering as they rode their Quarter horses around the farm.

However, as fate would have it, I seemed to have inherited my wariness of horses from my mother's side of the family, the Nelsons. My grandfather Nelson farmed with horses and rode in horse-drawn carriages but only out of necessity.

Horses also were a chief culprit in his father's drowning death. During a rainstorm at night, my great-grandfather was leading a horse-drawn carriage carrying his son and new bride (my grandfather and grandmother) across a small bridge at Cross's Ford after their wedding when he slipped and fell into the Iowa River.

Mom told me as soon as tractors and cars came on the scene, the horses disappeared. She never remembered him saddling up to ride one of the beasts. This family history did not work in my favor.

As I gazed at the best birthday present I had ever received, reality sent in. "I can't ride her until next April?" I grumbled.

My Dad shook his head, "No, better wait till May. You want to be sure she's strong enough to carry you." Little did he know those words were destined to be the best joke he had told in a long while.

He walked over, untied the rope that was tied to the pony's halter and started to lead her to a newly fenced in paddock. He stopped and looked at me. "What are you going to call her?"

I looked at the pretty white filly. She pricked her ears up as she waited to be led to her new enclosure. She looked more like a sheep than a pony. She had never been brushed in her young life so her coat was curly.

"Snowball," I announced. "I want to call her Snowball." My Dad nodded his approval. Mom just shook her head and went back into the house to work on my birthday cake.

I dutifully cared for Snowball throughout the rest of the fall, winter and early spring. I brushed, fed and watered her and made sure her small shed got scooped out. When May arrived, Dad saddled her and slipped a bridle on her for the first time. Snowball did not put up much of a fuss and let me lead her around.

After a few days of allowing her to get accustomed to the equipment, I started my efforts to break her. I never got to the riding part. Snowball allowed the saddle to be strapped to her back. She fidgeted with the bridle but didn't fight it. However, when I put any of my weight on her, she took off.

I don't mean a canter or trot, but she broke out into an all out run with a buck here and then. It didn't take long for the inexperienced cowboy — me — to be launched off her back. As soon as I hit the ground, she stopped and returned to grazing contentedly, only a few feet away.

She got trained all right — she learned how to literally get me off her back way before this phrase became slang.

Once or twice a week throughout the summer, I attempted to "saddle up," but it always ended up with boy down. My Dad would periodically ask how the riding was going. I'd tell him, and he would just shake his head. "Got to show her who's boss."

Oh, she knew all right. "Keep trying. You'll hang on one of these days." I think that's when the cynic in me started to develop.

As the year progressed, Snowball and I developed a love-hate relationship. She loved to be fed, brushed, petted and even stood still for hoof trimmings. She even came when called. For my part, I hated trying to ride her.

I ended my attempts at riding in the fall. That ground is hard when it's cold out, especially when you've landed on it butt first. Maybe that's why I relate to Charlie Brown in the Peanuts comic strip. When Lucy pulls the football away from Charlie after he tries to kick it — wham — he lands on the ground with a heavy thud.

Snowball made it through the following winter just fine. I made no attempts to ride her, and she repaid me by being a fairly docile little pony. She became just another livestock chore — feed, water and keep her bedding clean.

When the next spring rolled around, Dad inquired about my intentions with Snowball. "You going to ride that pony this year?" he asked in his typical undiplomatic way. "Better break her while you can ride her."

Of course, no help was offered. Horsemanship was in my blood, right? I just had to channel my inner Roy Rogers. Well, Roy was no help either.

That year, I stepped up my efforts to ride her, and she developed the meanest and most determined methods to shed me from her back. I will try to remember some of her more creative moves. I may have bonked my head a few times so I probably have forgotten a few episodes.

The white beast thought she could just run and buck me off. I was bigger and stronger and determined to hang on. So, she found other effective measures.

Snowball scraped me off by running under the clothes line. Of course, the line struck me squarely in the throat and I was jettisoned off. I think I was able to speak again after a day or two.

Our front yard contained three good-sized trees — a bur oak, walnut and pine — and Snowball learned that pesky weight could be scraped off if she collided with them at full gallop.

Another trick was to rear on her hind legs, sending me crashing to the ground. I learned what having the "wind knocked out you" feels like.

For a few seconds you feel like you're dying until you cough oxygen back into your lungs.

One Sunday, a visiting cousin offered his help with the white tornado. He was a wrestler and about my age. His family owned a horse, which he rode occasionally. But, his steed was a well-trained, docile Quarter horse.

"That's what's giving you trouble?" Cousin Gary asked a bit skeptically as he watched the peaceful Shetland grazing nearby.

I nodded. "Yep. Go for it." A smile flickered across his face as he approached her. He stroked her mane for a few seconds then sprang on her back. Snowball took off like her tail was on fire. I had never seen her move that fast. Gary's arms and legs flailed wildly as he tried to get her under control, but she had zeroed in on a target — a nearby barn door.

The pony turned at the last second and smacked Gary into the door at full run. She caromed off the barn and Gary bounced off her back, landing with a splat on the ground. Snowball stopped immediately and returned to grazing, no worse for wear.

I ran over to Gary, who gingerly rose to his feet and brushed himself off. "You OK?" I asked.

He nodded but looked at Snowball with a lot more respect. "How often does she do that?" he asked, shaking his head.

I shrugged. "That was a new one. She usually runs into trees or just bucks 'till I fall off."

Gary looked at me and shook his head. "I'm not doing that again!"

I nodded. "I know what you mean." We returned Snowball to her pen and went off to play a gentler sport — football.

Later that summer, I tried to ride Snowball one more time. Even though I had been riding my bike everywhere and was having fun racing the neighbor kids up and down the country roads, unfinished business with that pony still gnawed on me. Well, that and the occasional question from Dad wondering how the training was coming.

I approached Snowball cautiously and brushed her for a bit. She actually liked attention and would stand perfectly still without being tied up. I gradually leaned on her back. Snowball pinned her ears back for a second but waited. I brushed her some more and put more weight on her — nothing.

With Charlie Brown-like optimism, I grabbed the bridle reins and swung my right leg over her back and grabbed on tight. She started to walk slowly and then galloped towards a nearby outbuilding. I managed to pull her back and avoided the collision. She snorted and started to run, but I reined her in.

Now it was "go" time. Snowball bucked then ran and bucked some more. I hung on. She broke into a full run and stopped suddenly. I hung on. By this time, her ears were fully laid back on her head — not a good sign.

Snowball started to run in a circle, snorting and throwing her head up and down. I still hung on, though I shouldn't have. She launched herself into the air and writhed in a move that would have made a rodeo bronc proud. Somehow, I still clung to her.

She then did something I've never seen another horse do. Snowball reared straight up on her hind legs. I stayed put but started to slip. The next part seems like it took place in slow motion.

I remember falling to the ground, landing on my back and seeing legs and hooves sail over my head. Snowball had tipped over and fallen backwards. I'm not sure how she didn't land on me, but she didn't and hit the ground with a thud, rolled over, snorted, walked a few feet away and started grazing as if it was business as usual.

Dazed, I sat up and checked myself. Just some bruises — no broken bones. I shook my head and looked at my nemesis. The both of us had just flipped over backwards and neither was injured. I made up mind right then and there that I didn't need to ride her that badly.

Little did I know that Snowball had declared war. Later than day, I was hurrying through chores probably trying finish in time to catch a TV show. I made the mistake of feeding Snowball first and was crossing through her pen to save time. She was eating when I walked behind her — big mistake.

I don't remember the kick but a hoof hit me squarely in the worst possible place. I went down like a prize fighter who just had his bell rung. Snowball wasn't finished. I lay there for a bit and tried to get up when I heard what sounded like a hammer striking an anvil. Snowball had kicked again and hit the metal fence post just above my head.

Seeing the commotion, my dog and loyal companion Charlie charged over and barked furiously at the pony. She turned and kicked but only hit the fence. Good old Charlie backed up and charged a second time. Snowball kick again but missed her target. I gathered what strength I had and vaulted over the fence, landing in a fetal position on the ground.

With the intruder gone, Snowball returned to feeding. Not feeling well, I started to crawl on my hands and knees to the house, which was about thirty yards or so away. Charlie saw this as an invitation to play. He lowered his head and collided with me, smacking me in the ribs. Damn dog!

Charlie and I used to wrestle. I would throw him to he ground — not hard — and the both of us would roll around until one of us got tired of the game. It was usually me. Now Charlie thought I was in the wrestling stance, and he wanted to play. The dog stopped harassing me when I finally could muster enough energy to yell at him in loud and obscene terms to leave me alone.

Hearing the commotion, Dad came to investigate and found me still crawling toward the house. He had heard the barking and his youngest son screaming some very unpleasant phrases. "What happened?"

I pointed to Snowball and gasped, "She kicked me." I continued crawling toward the house.

"Are you going to be all right?" At this moment, Mom came out to check on the situation. I assured both I was OK, finally got to my feet and stumbled toward the house.

"Where you going?" Dad asked.

I kept walking but croaked, "To get my gun. Going to shoot that damn pony. Last time she kicks anyone!"

Mom and Dad eventually talked me out of my assassination plot, and I limped into the house. Two days later Snowball was gone. Dad sold her to someone who wanted a team of all white ponies he could hitch to a wagon and show off in parades. He wanted Snowball as a brood mare to help achieve this goal.

I didn't see Snowball go and didn't care. Good riddance.

Years later, during a family reunion, Gary and I were catching up on old times. It had been years since we'd seen each other. He turned to me during a lull in the conversation. "Whatever happened to that pony of yours? She was mean!"

My oldest daughter interrupted with a laugh. "Do you mean those stories are true? She was really that bad?"

Gary and I looked at her and simply said, "Yep."

9
Chore Boy

One fact of life is common with every kid who grew up on a working farm — chores.

These duties varied with every farm. In 1960s-'70's Iowa, you could find every kind of operation imaginable just driving around a four-mile square of country roads — dairy, beef, hogs, sheep, all grain or a combination of all of those. We raised beef cattle and hogs.

Thankfully, Mom and Dad sold the milk cows after my brothers grew up and left home. Being the "tail-ender" by a long ways in the family of four boys, I was spared being rousted out of bed at the ungodly hour of 4:30 or 5 a.m. to milk cows.

I heard stories of what a "character-building" experience it was to be kicked, stepped on or swatted in the face by a manure-caked tail while milking by hand.

My character developed just fine — thank you — from other experiences, such as escaping from angry cows or bulls, dodging the snapping jaws of sows, walking beans, haying and picking up rocks out of fields. You get the picture.

At about age 10, I was "anointed" to be the afternoon chore boy. Dad didn't mind being in charge of the morning routine. He could take his time feeding and inspecting the livestock to be sure his young indentured servant — yours, truly — was doing his job correctly. I had to catch the school bus, which usually scooped me up at about 7:45, so this arrangement worked well for both of us.

Our livestock operation was spread over a fairly large area. Most of the sows and their litters had run of a 10-acre pasture. Now, this was perfect for the hogs, since they had plenty of room to roam, forage, wallow and snooze under some large oaks.

It was not ideal for a skinny farm kid who had to lug feed and sometimes water by hand to feed the hungry mothers and their babies.

Of course, this pasture was on the opposite side of the farmstead from where the feed was stored.

I learned to move quickly when distributing feed to avoid being knocked over by the large, hungry mothers hurrying to gobble their second meal of the day. Many years later, when I was being treated by a chiropractor for lower back pain, he just nodded and said, "A farm kid, huh? Yeah, I've seen a lot these problems."

When the pigs were weaned from their mothers, we used several types of feeders. The most iconic of these was a small stainless-steel unit. The feeder had a tank with a lid on top. On either side of the feeder were four individual feeding stations with lids.

The lids were efficient in two ways. They kept the feed, usually a ground-up corn-and-mineral mixture, dry from the elements and reduced spillage.

To train the young pigs to eat from the feeder, Dad would tie the lids open for a day or two. After that, the lids came down. It didn't take long for the hungry and resourceful youngsters to learn to flip open the lid, stick their head in and eat until they were satisfied.

Of course, when departing from the feeder, the lid would crash down with a resounding metallic clank. This sound soon became part of the daily farmyard symphony. It was common to fall asleep on summer nights, when the windows were open, to the steady bang, bang, bang of those feeders.

When the pigs got older, they were switched to a larger self feeder. The 10-foot tall, A-frame wood building was open on both sides with feeding stations where the animals could dine.

Each side of the feeder had a trap door just below the point of the roof. My job was to get a six-foot wooden ladder that was attached below the door, climb up and use a long pole to loosen the powder-like feed so it would flow into the feed slots.

Usually after a rain or a typical hot and humid Iowa summer day, the feed would be clumped. It would take quite a few swipes with the pole and a lot of colorful language to get the feed to obey gravity.

When that chore was done, the doors, ladder and pole would get fastened back into place and one sweaty farm boy, who looked like he had rolled around in talcum powder, would trudge up to the house to wash off.

Bringing up the cow herd in the late afternoon was the most time-consuming and potentially dangerous chore. Every morning and afternoon, we either led the cows down to or herded them back home from a 30-acre pasture, located about a tenth of a mile down the gravel road past our farmstead.

In the late afternoon, I walked down to the pasture accompanied by my "body guard," Charlie the wonder dog. Our small herd of Black Angus would be swarmed around the gate like elementary school kids ready to spring out the doors when the dismissal bell rang.

If the farm pond had water in it, the cows took their time to saunter home. However, if the pond had dried up in the August sun, the cows were looking forward to dipping their muzzles into the stock tank.

Sometimes, the herd would back up if I yelled. Often, I had to order Charlie to "sic 'em," just to get them to back off a few feet so I could unhook the gate, swing it open and get the heck out of the way.

Bringing the cattle home was a two-person job. Most often, Mom would get recruited to stand at the top of the hill, which led to our farmstead, to warn any oncoming cars to slow down and not spook the beasts.

On a good day, the herd would follow the Boss Cow up the hill, turn left into the driveway and take an immediate right into the paddock and make a beeline for the water tank. For years, the herd's leader was an unusual looking cow. She was coal black like the rest of herd but resembled a Holstein, being bigger and possessing an udder twice the size of the other cows.

Dad told me Boss Cow was a holdover from my grandfather's milk herd. She was the product of a Holstein mother and Angus sire. It was common to see an extra calf nursing from her generous milk supply. Almost all the females in our herd were her daughters, granddaughters or great-granddaughters.

On a bad day during the daily roundup, either a spooky heifer, new mother or contrary bull would refuse to leave the premises.

I don't know which of those situations I disliked most. For some reason, the spooked animals would turn tail and run to the opposite end of the pasture. Even Charlie would like at me like he was saying: "Really? I suppose you want me to go chase her back to the barn?" It usually took several unsuccessful tries before the runaway cooperated and returned home.

Dealing with bulls was always hazardous duty. Sometimes a young male would bellow and paw the ground. Not a good sign. On my command, Charlie would charge after the bull, which in turn would try to stomp the barking white tornado nipping at his heels. The bull's attempted defense was futile.

After a few rounds of playing "sic 'em," the bull usually lost his bravado and trotted home. I have to admit, once in a while I let Charlie pester a pain-in-the-butt male all the way back to the paddock just to let him know who was boss.

A new mother was a different story. The cow usually stayed away from the rest of the herd, mooed anxiously and paced back and forth nervously. When this happened, I closed the gate and waited until I got reinforcements.

This usually entailed Dad and I taking the pickup to the pasture to find the newborn. Somehow, we would distract the mother — Charlie was good at that — and lift the wobbly calf into the cargo bed. Dad would hold the calf, while I slowly drove back up the road, followed by the anxious mother.

When we'd get back home, Dad would gently lift the calf out, put it on the ground and let the mother take over. Just another day on the farm.

10
The King and Queens

Cats have always been a valuable asset on a farm. If the operation has livestock, then feed is stored nearby which attracts rodents. One only has to see a cat in action hunting or see its trophies proudly presented at your feet or on a doorstep to appreciate the domestic tiger has been on patrol.

Our farm was no different. Cats were everywhere. They were all sizes, colors and hair lengths. They were always outdoor cats. We had two barns usually full of hay and/or straw that also housed livestock. The cats found plenty of shelter and warmth there.

My mother did not like animals in the house. Once in a while she allowed me to bring in a favorite cat for an hour or two to sit on my lap while watching TV. But that's as far as it got. The cat was always shooed back outside over night.

When I was getting old enough to venture outside on my own, our cats became one of my favorite pastimes. However, when I was 5 or 6 years old, our farm cats were stricken with some kind of malady that made them all sickly. The kittens' eyes were always matted over. All the felines were lethargic and gaunt.

One fall day, the cats disappeared — all of them. Being a little guy, I accepted my parents' explanation that the cats all got sick and died at the same time. It's funny, but I never questioned them about it. Farm kids all know animals do not live forever. My parents told me much later they thought it was distemper. I don't know if they were gathered up and euthanized or if one of my brothers — obviously the one who disliked felines — was given carte blanche to use them for target practice.

~ Mathilda ~

After the great exodus (or execution) of 1958/59, it was a full year before another cat was allowed on the place. Strays or wandering neighbor cats disappeared quickly — probably thanks to my target-shooting brother. Due to that fact, I suspect my family wanted to make sure whatever triggered the disease had dissipated. I got through the year without felines, but I'm sure I begged constantly for a cat.

One spring day, my parents told me we were going to visit our neighbors, the Walthalls. I needed no convincing. Edna was always kind and either had homemade candy or cookies at the ready, and Milo was a kind man with a loud, boisterous laugh.

It only took a couple of minutes to get to their farm. We could see their buildings from our dining room window. When we arrived, a smiling Milo gestured for me to follow him to the barn. Once inside, I just stood there with my mouth open. Kittens skittered everywhere. They were on the hay bales, climbing up the rafters, drinking from pans of milk or nursing from their mothers. Every color of cat imaginable was represented.

I had never seen healthy kittens before. They had bright eyes and were scampering about, rolling and play fighting with each other. I looked at Milo. "Can I hold one?"

He erupted with one of his signature guffaws. "Sure, but you better take one of them home." I looked up at my parents. They just smiled and nodded. Dad was more of a dog guy, but he tolerated cats. Mom loved cats. As an only child growing up on the farm where we now lived, cats were one of her chief playthings.

I plopped down on the straw-covered floor and watched the kittens play. Some of them ran by. A few stopped to let me pet them but then they were off to play with their litter mates.

One kitten scampered over to me and started to play with my shoestrings. It was a pretty female with golden eyes. Her brown coat was splashed with yellow spots. We incorrectly described her as a calico. It was years later when I learned her particular coloring was called tortoise shell.

The kitten rolled over and let me pet her tummy. She play boxed with my hands but kept her claws retracted. Dad asked if the mother was a good mouser. Milo nodded.

"I want this one!" I declared.

"What are you going to name her?" Mom asked.

I picked up the purring kitten. "Mathilda!" I announced. The three adults turned in unison and looked at me. Mom and Milo smiled. Dad just shook his head.

"Where did that come from?" Mom asked.

"She looks like a Mathilda," I answered. To this day, I have no idea where that name came to mind. We didn't know anyone by that name. I can't remember hearing it before. The name just seemed right.

The kitten didn't care what it was called. All of our cats would come to "here kitty, kitty." Names didn't seem to matter to a cat. So, Mathilda came home with us and became queen of the farm.

All of our cats were good hunters, and Mathilda was no exception. I witnessed this first hand. One day, while doing some chores in the barn, I sat down to pat her. She curled up in my lap and started purring.

A short time later, two male sparrows started sparring. They loudly chirped and fluttered at each other. Their brawl soon took them down to the barn floor about 10 feet away from us. Mathilda sprang from my lap and was on the sparrows in three bounds. One of the combatants became her lunch and the other shakily flew up to a perch and escaped out a window.

After the sparrow incident, I felt a burning sensation on my legs. Dropping my jeans, I discovered three long red lines running down my inner thighs. Mathilda had gone full-claws-out when she attacked the sparrows. This was the only time she ever scratched me.

The queen became the mother, grandmother and great-grandmother of every cat on our farm. The gentle female proved to be extremely fertile as well as a dutiful mother. Mathilda would sneak away and hide in the most out-of-the-way places.

I found more nooks and crannies when trying to follow her to find her kittens. She raised more live kittens than any other mother cat I have ever seen. Within a few years of Mathilda's reign as queen mother, we had more cats than we knew what to do with. It was rare when she lost a kitten and when she did, it usually was a tragic event.

One summer night when Mathilda was 3 or 4 years old, she came running over to me, frantically circled my legs, meowed loudly, ran toward the barn and stopped to look back at me. Curious by her strange behavior, I followed her into our small barn and up into one of side lofts.

Mathilda was circling a pile of four maybe one-week-old kittens. Her dead babies were all missing their heads. That was the tell-tale sign of a tom-cat killing. It was probably a stray male passing through intent on killing kittens not sired by him and thus causing a female to go into heat a short time later.

The distraught mother growled, sniffed at her kittens and hissed. She repeated this behavior over and over, then circled my legs and meowed. There was nothing I could do for her or the kittens.

Our tom cat and protector of kittens at the time — a fierce little male who effectively drove away all strange toms — had been exiled from the farm (dumped three or four miles away) for sucking eggs, a crime in my Dad's eyes.

This was the only time I had seen Mathilda beg for help. I sat down feeling sad and angry. Mathilda continued her circling, growling and hissing. I tried to pet her, but she would not stay still. Since there was nothing I could do, I left the mother to her mourning. I buried the babies the next day.

About a week later, I was hunting pigeons near the barn when I heard a cat yowling. Not recognizing which feline was making the noise, I crept into barn and quietly climbed into the loft. A strange buff-colored tom sat on a bale and stared warily at me. He was only about twenty feet from where Mathilda's kittens had been killed. I slowly raised my .22 bolt-action rifle and fired.

I never liked killing domestic animals for whatever reason, but I have to admit a certain satisfaction for exterminating a kitten killer. I left the body where it lay as a warning to any other stray. Later that summer, our tom returned looking a bit bedraggled but otherwise healthy. As far as I'm aware, no other kittens died on his watch.

~ Tommy ~

One spring day when I was playing with Mathilda's first litter of kittens, I noticed a pretty gray tiger cat watching us from the nearby barn door. The strange tom had a white patch than ran from his nose to his chest. His white paws made it look he was wearing boots. He regarded me casually but moved away when I approached.

For about a week whenever I checked on the kittens, the tom was there, too. Mathilda did not seem to mind. She brought the kittens rodents and peacefully nursed them with him standing guard. He waited his turn during feeding time, letting the kittens and Mathilda eat first.

Each day, the smallish male inched a bit closer. The tom watched curiously as the kittens would run around me in a game of tag and jump in my lap to be petted. After one particularly playful episode with the kittens, the tom approached me and sort of meowed. His soft voice was more of a rasp. It sounded something like: whaanh.

I'm not sure why, but I imitated him — whaanh. We conversed several times then, without warning, he walked over and let me pet him. He rubbed against me and then returned to his sentry duty. The male looked like he was about a year old. I do not know how he found our farm. Perhaps he came from a nearby farm and was driven off by a bigger tom.

His naming ceremony was much less formal than Mathilda's. He was a tom, a small one at that so I brilliantly named him Tommy. In retrospect, he should have been named King or Tiger. As mentioned earlier, very few if any kittens were killed by stray males when he was on patrol. More than once in the spring, I'd awaken to yowling, screeching cat fights.

Usually the next morning, Tommy would be perched on one of the cement steps, enjoying the sun and patiently waiting to be fed. Once in awhile, his nose bore a scratch after a skirmish but he kept relatively unscathed.

One of these brawls happened during the daytime. I heard a raucous — screeching and howling, not unlike banshees — coming from one of our corn cribs. When I peeked in, Tommy had a stray male trapped up the side and in a corner of a roof rafter.

The hapless visitor was almost the twice the size of his small tiger tormentor and was screeching in fear. Tommy's ears were pinned back to his head and his tail was whipping about like an angry snake. His growl was impressively vicious sounding.

The stray finally figured enough was enough and jumped about 10 feet to the floor. I swear Tommy did a back flip, landing perfectly and chased the other cat out of the crib and into a nearby corn field. He returned a short time later — no worse for wear — walked over to me and rubbed himself on my legs. Now that was a good cat.

As fearsome as he was with stray males, Tommy was incredibly patient with kittens. Sometimes the overly enthusiastic babies would play attack his twitching tail. He'd tolerate a few swipes at his tail then bat at the kitten with a sheathed paw and walk away. If the youngster persisted in its pestering, Tommy would end the play with two or three cuffs to the head. Even the dullest kitten got that message.

More than once I saw him reach out, grab a kitten and lick its face, almost in a paternal gesture. Perhaps he was marking the kittens with his scent. In a sense, protecting them. I have never seen another tom do that — not even his sons and grandsons. At best our other toms ignored kittens.

I was the only one "allowed" to pet him. He did not like to be picked up. I found that out the hard way when I tried to carry him one day. He writhed and struggled with his claws unsheathed in an effort to escape. Though he was small (probably about 6 pounds), Tommy was all muscle.

Like Mathilda, he only scratched me once, but he left me a souvenir of his displeasure with bloody lines across my chest and stomach. I never picked him up after that.

As mentioned earlier, Tommy committed the sin — in Dad's eyes — of sucking chicken eggs. Basically, he must have found there was tasty liquid inside eggs. Dad may have found him lapping up a broken egg and issued the sentence of banishment.

Without my knowing, Dad threw Tommy in a bag, drove "a few miles" (his words) away across the nearby Iowa River and dumped him a short distance from another farm. I hope he wore gloves because I don't think that cat would have gone peacefully. Dad finally told me what he'd done when I noticed Tommy hadn't shown up for a couple of suppers — unusual for him.

I was not happy about Dad being judge, jury and enforcement officer but the deed was done. Not long after that, a litter of Mathilda's kittens was killed by a stray tom and several of our other cats — young males — came up missing. Even the other female cats acted skittish with the loss of their protector. However, that determined little male was not to be denied.

Later that summer, maybe two months after Tommy was exiled, I was talking to Mom in the yard when she stopped and smiled. I paid no attention when one of our cats rubbed against my legs. I only looked down when the rubbing persisted. There he was, looking a bit gaunt with some weed stickers clinging in his coat — Tommy!

I'm not sure how many lives the cat used up to make it home, but he found his way. Even Dad was impressed and assured me Tommy could stay no matter how many eggs he ate.

~ Fluff ~

I had two buddies who accompanied me on hunts — my second dog, Ben, and Fluff, a small yellow female cat. Fluff was one of Mathilda's daughters, probably from her first or second litter. When Mom first saw the long-haired kitten she likened her to a ball of fluff. Another name stuck.

Like her mother, Fluff was a good mother and expert hunter. She learned early on when I came back from hunting, I often brought back a squirrel, rabbit or pigeon and would give them to the mother cats who would carry the fresh kills to their babies.

It didn't take Fluff long to associate me walking out of the house with one of my guns with a potential tasty entree. Our large barn was a favorite nesting and roosting place for pigeons. Many times, when I would see the birds perched on the roof, I'd grab my .410-gauge (small) shotgun and try to sneak up on them. Or if I heard them cooing inside the barn, I'd take my BB gun into the loft in an attempt to pick one off.

During these forays, Fluff usually followed close behind me, tail up in excited expectation. She'd wait patiently until she heard the bang from the shotgun or ping from the BB gun and rush over to grab a dying or wounded bird.

One time, when I climbed into the loft with her on my heels, I missed the pigeon I was aiming at. My target and all the other members of its flock escaped out the barn window.

Hearing the familiar ping and the fluttering of wings, Fluff ran around the loft looking for a downed bird. After a minute or two, she looked at me as if saying, "Well, Davy Crockett, where's my lunch?"

I just shrugged and told her, "I missed." Yes, I talked to a cat. She sat there for another moment and I swear she looked at me with disappointment, turned her back and left me alone to think about the error of my ways.

Fluff's love of hunting unfortunately caused her to lose quite a few kittens. When her babies reached about two months old, she would take them on hunting trips into our 20-acre timber. Sadly, Fluff often left with four or five youngsters and came back two or three. I don't know what happened but suspect the kittens either got lost or fell prey to owls, raccoons or any number of other predators that lived in the woods. It was not uncommon for Fluff to raise one kitten to adulthood whereas Mathilda saw most of her kitten grow up.

~ Road Trip ~

About five or six years after the re-introduction of cats on our farm, our place was over run by the progeny of Mathilda and Tommy. Even I lost count. It was easy keeping track with one or two mother cats, but now Mathilda's daughters, granddaughters and great-granddaughters were happily spreading their genetics. Tommy usually chased the young toms — most likely his sons and grandsons — away.

At one feeding, I counted more than 25 cats enjoying our dining facilities. Mom and Dad allowed me my pastimes, but this growing "clowder" (herd) of cats was too much. My parents did not appreciate feeding that many felines and also feared that many cats would attract a return of distemper.

Dad sat me down and told me had called the veterinary school at Iowa State University in Ames, which was about 50 miles south of where we lived. The vet clinic had agreed to take our cats for its research programs.

Yes, that sounds terrible. But, at the time, I didn't understand the full ramification of what that testing meant.

The day of the culling was a sad day event. I was told that most of the cats that were two years old and younger were destined for Ames. Mathilda, Tommy and Fluff would be spared. I only was allowed to keep three of the younger cats. Talk about a heart-rending moment.

We fed the cats, and Dad brought out two portable chicken coops. I paroled two pretty grays and an almost white one and the rest were stuffed into the carriers.

A half-grown tom — a gray tiger, imagine that — fought his way out and escaped. All totaled, we collected 20-some cats. Dad stuffed the coops into the trunk of our car and we drove to Ames while being serenaded by some very irritated felines.

When we got to the vet school, Dad hauled the coops out and asked where they wanted the cats. One of the staffers foolishly said to let them out and they would take care of them.

I looked at Dad and said, "I don't think that's a good idea." He nodded but complied with the staffer's request and slid the doors open. I've never seen an explosion of cats like that before or since. The scared felines bolted out of their cramped prison cages like uncoiled springs. They ran, climbed and hid everywhere.

The last thing I remember of that scene was Dad and I backing out of the lab. Another vet staffer stared in horror as one of our cats clawed its way up his pant leg. The ride back home was sullen and quiet. Even Mom and Dad didn't talk, and I sniffled most of the way. I hope those cats' sacrifice was put to good use.

~ No Goodbyes ~

I have not related the end of the lives of my favorite three cats — Mathilda, Tommy and Fluff — for good reason. I don't know. The hard truth about most farm cats is that they are born and die in secret. The average life of a farm cat is about five or six years. They are at risk from the elements, disease, other predators and vehicles.

All three of these cats at least lived an average life span. Fluff outlived the other two and was quite the old lady when she finally succumbed. Spring was not always a happy event. Eventually, there came a time when my cats didn't show up to be fed. I would wait for a week or two and sadly concede that I'd never see them again.

I hope Mathilda died peacefully curled up snug and warm wedged between some straw bales. Fluff may have finally been cornered during one of her hunting trips. And, if Tommy finally fell to a younger, fiercer male, I'm sure he didn't give up without one hell of a fight.

~ The Heirs ~

When Fluff was nearing the end of her life, I no longer was involved with the farm. After high school, I headed off to college and lost track of the cats. I got glimpses of them during visits, but the felines didn't know me, and they were not tame enough to be petted. After I left, my parents continued to feed whatever cats showed up.

Mathilda, Tommy and Fluff left a lineage that lasted at least 40 years. The cat family tree was easy to trace by the maternal line:

Mathilda (tortoise shell)
Fluff (yellow, long haired)
Princess (tortoise shell named by Dad)
gray tiger mother
white mother one
white mother two
unknown mother
black mother one and
black mother two (named Mama Cat by my brother, Roger).

The only son of Tommy that lived at our farm was born the spring his sire disappeared. He was a beautiful gray tiger with a white chest and white legs. We called him Boots.

This young male would have been better off being a house cat. He inherited none of Tommy's fighting spirit. He was continuously tortured and chased up trees by stray toms, perhaps by other sons or grandsons of Tommy come back to reclaim their territory. Though not a fighter, to his credit, Boots refused to be driven away. I suspect he lived long enough to father the first white mother cat.

In 1999, my brother announced he was selling the farmstead and moving back to the West Coast. My brothers and I had sold the farmland to a neighbor in 1997 after Mom passed away.

I was taking one last look around the place when I spotted Mama Cat nursing some kittens near one of our outbuildings. I snuck around to the other side and quietly approached. To my delight, she was feeding a rainbow clutch, which included a tortoise shell, a gray with white paws and two black kittens. It could not have a been a better going away gift.

11
Tasty Reward

This story is written in honor of Myrlyn Bartling Sr. A friend and neighbor who died in a farm accident.

A lot of kids, when I was growing up, probably got a sip of beer early on when their dad or another relative cracked open a Miller, Bud, Hamm's or Grain Belt (if they were unlucky) and let them have a sip. Other youngsters belonged to a church where wine is served at communion so they had a little experience with the fruit of the grape.

Not so in my family. I was raised by a tee-totaling old-fashioned Methodist mother. I know Dad had a sip or two with his buddies when he ran errands into town or attended Saturday night sales at the local auction house.

However, for most of my life, booze of any kind was forbidden in the house. In later years, Mom finally looked the other way when Dad stored his Mogen David in a Log Cabin maple syrup container.

So, even getting the chance to taste a beer, let alone drink one before age 21 was not looking like a possibility. My first "cold one" came at an unplanned, casual but defining moment.

When farm youths reach their mid-teen years they are sought after for hired help, whether it was for hay/straw baling, driving tractors, walking beans, helping with extra chores, shelling corn or milking. I was no exception.

One of our neighbors — Myrlyn Bartling Sr. — did custom corn shelling with his brother, Jim. They often required extra help when they were in the middle of a job. This usually entailed a crew of men and boys to climb in a crib filled with corn and rake and/or shovel the ears into the augers or conveyors.

The corn then would flow into the sheller which did as its name indicates — separate the kernels from the cob. The kernels would fill up a hopper and the cobs would be spit out of a spout and slowly grow into an impressive mountain.

The kernels then most likely would be ground up and mixed with minerals for livestock feed. The cobs could be used for livestock bedding or a fuel source. Dad burned them in a metal box attached to our livestock waterers in the winter to prevent the water from freezing.

During one early fall day, the Bartlings needed a few bodies to help with a shelling crew at a neighbor's farm. Since Dad was busy with a truck-hauling job, I got volunteered for the duty. I probably grumbled a bit but showed up at the requested time.

Corn shelling could be an adventure depending on what kind of crib you were dealing with. This particular crib looked like a small slatted barn with a drive-through alleyway. Ears were stored in both sides of the building. Part of the job was to keep the ears flowing into the conveyor. This meant someone or a few guys had to crawl up on top of the pile of ears and keep them flowing. Often, mini ear slides would ensue which meant the laborer had to ride the moving pile down and catch himself at the bottom.

The job needed able bodies to keep raking and shoveling the ears into the conveyor. One other experience that sprang from shelling was the hordes of mice and rats that frequently ran out during the emptying of a crib.

Many veteran shellers tied their pant legs shut to keep the varmints from finding an unpleasant path to freedom. I never witnessed this but heard stories about more than one old farmer doing a pant-leg shaking, war-hoop dance after one of the critters invaded his privacy.

Despite the constant grinding and rumble of the corn sheller, dogs and cats soon learned that rodents galore gushed out of all this commotion. The pets would patrol nearby and rush over to either pounce on or scoop up an escapee in their jaws. All this activity made for a long and hectic day.

About half-way through the job, a bit after lunch, Dad drove over to the neighbor's place and offered to take my place on the shelling line. I looked at him and one thought went through my mind: "Nope, I'm going to show these guys I can work as hard as they can."

My reaction was caused by recent conversation with one of my buddies, an ex farm kid. He asked me one time why it took me so long to start working on the farm. Talk among the local gossipers was that Mom wanted to protect the last of her sons. Not so. I was "working" — doing chores, running errands and driving tractors — on the farm since I was 9 or 10 years old.

The neighbors just didn't "see" me being active until I was about 12 and starting to drive a tractor back and forth to the fields. I was not one of those tag-along farm boys who were climbing all over machinery when they 8 years old.

What was surprising to me was my friend grew up about 12 miles away, and four years later the wags were still talking about it. Really?

I turned to Dad and said, "No, I'm fine. I'll finish up here and come home when we're done." He looked surprised but just nodded and drove back home. I could see the other guys in the crew watching our conversation out of the corners of their eyes.

A bit later, the neighbor whose place we were working at sauntered over. "Decided to give the old man a break, eh?" he said with a twinkle in his eye.

I nodded. "Yep, figured he'd like to go home and get a nap." This brought guffaws from my co-workers. The shelling crew finished in the late afternoon. No one reported a pants-leg incident, but we saw plenty of rodents scurrying away.

We found a cool spot under a huge oak tree and plopped on the ground. The other guys and I were tired and sweaty. The itchy dust was everywhere — in our hair, up our noses, down our shirts and pants. Everywhere.

As we sat there enjoying the cool breeze. I saw Myrlyn doling out beer to the rest of the crew. Then, without saying a word, he nonchalantly handed me a bottle, popped the cap off with a hand-held opener and sat down to join us. No one said a word. I looked at the bottle and took a swig.

I don't remember what was on the label. I was tired and hot, and the beer was cold. It tasted good. I appreciated the gesture for a job well done. Though I didn't tell her at the time, I think even Mom would have approved.

Vignette III. Redundancies

I may have grown up with one of the easiest addresses to remember:
> Williams Family
> Rural Route 2
> Hardin Township
> Hardin County
> Iowa Falls, Iowa. (Pre ZIP code)

No wonder I had our address memorized soon after starting school. Now, the phone number was another issue. It started out promising enough — 515 (at the time) — but went downhill from there with a random set of digits and no repeats. What were they thinking? I finally got it, but it took a lot longer for me to repeat it back to anyone.

Mom and I both found the redundancies in our address to be funny. I remember the first time she explained it to me. I think I looked at her and said: "Really? That's it?" She smiled and tested me.

"Now repeat it back to me," said Mom, a former school teacher. I repeated it back accurately.

Then she tried to trick me. "OK, what state do we live in?"

"Iowa," I said correctly.

"What township?"

"Hardin," I answered.

"What's our address?" she asked, squinting at me thoughtfully.

"Uh, Iowa Fa … Nope, Route 2," I said smiling.

"Rural Route 2," she corrected, emphasizing the word "rural." I winced. There was that same foreign-sounding guttural utterance that had tripped me up the first day of kindergarten class. (See Tough First Day in this collection.) I repeated it back again, and she nodded her approval.

"What county?" she fired at me.

"Hardin?" I answered a bit hesitantly.

She smiled and asked: "What town do we put on our address?"

Hmm, was she trying to trick me again? We actually lived closer to Owasa but that didn't sound right. I thought through the whole litany of our address and blurted out: "Iowa Falls!"

"Good!" Mom declared. "Now let's work on the phone number."

Uh-oh.

12
Party Line

"Don't answer that phone! Didn't you hear the three short rings?" My mother admonished me when I raced over to pick up the receiver on our black rotary telephone that was attached to the dining room wall.

As a youngster, I didn't notice the difference between our neighbor's three short rings and the two long rings which meant it was a call for our house. Like most folks living out of city limits in the 1940s through 1960s, we had a party line.

Several families shared a phone line. When the phone rang, you had to listen to the duration of rings. Three shorts meant someone was calling the Rush family — very nice people. If the phone sounded out two longs, a certain farm boy actually got a chance to talk to someone in the outside world.

If I remember correctly, we could call six neighbors by using just three digits. For example, we could dial something like 570 to call the Rushes or 571 for the Warrens and so on.

The party line often lived up to its name. At any time during a call, a neighbor could pick up the receiver and listen to the conversation. You could almost always hear the tell-tale click in the receiver, then the reception got a little weaker.

Let's just say some folks abused this feature by eavesdropping on your conversation. I'm told folks in Dubuque County called this practice "rubbering."

You had to be careful what you said, especially if it was a sensitive subject you were discussing because the whole neighborhood would be gossiping about it before the day was over.

One neighbor lady was well known for her three-click warning that she wanted to use the telephone. My parents would shake their heads and say something to the impatient Mabel (not her real name) like:

"We'll be off the line in a minute or we just started talking, check back in a few minutes." Mabel also was the chief eavesdropping perpetrator.

Dad actually was the more diplomatic parent, at least on the phone. One time Mabel tried interrupting a call from one of my brothers, who was serving overseas in the Army.

Mom would not stand for it. "Whoever is on the line, get off! This is a LONG DISTANCE call from my son and he only has few minutes to talk!" Telling someone you were on a long-distance call usually was code for "important" or a private family matter.

If the uninvited listener stayed on the line during one of these overseas calls, Mom would get serious. Usually those military calls only lasted about three minutes so time was precious.

"Mabel, if that's you, hang up now or we will have a long talk later!" Even Mabel knew not to cross Mom. She may not have won many diplomatic points, but you knew where you stood with Mom.

Sometimes my military brothers would call "collect." When you answered the phone, an operator would say, "You have a collect call from (so and so), will you accept the charges?" Meaning, will you pay for the call?

I hung up on an operator only once when I was a youngster and never did it again after getting a lecture.

"Who was on the phone?" Mom asked when I listened in the receiver and jammed it hurriedly back on the hook.

"I don't know. Some lady wanted to charge me for doing something. Someone was yelling in the background not to hang up, but it scared me."

Mom rushed over. "Oh for heaven's sake, that must have been a collect call. Don't ever do that again!" Those were strong words from Mom. Her language and threats evolved as I got older.

Usually, the operator called back within a minute, and Mom handled the transaction.

One time the phone rang during supper when I was an older teenager. It was three shorts. I was sitting closest to the phone. Ring, ring, ring ... ring, ring, ring ... ring, ring, ring ... ring, ring ring. I counted 12 times. Usually, callers gave up after six rings. If a person was in the house, six rings gave them plenty of time to pick up the phone. After that, guess what? Your intended "callee" was outside or not home.

After two more sets of three rings, I jumped up, grabbed the phone and snarled, "For Pete's sake, they're not home. Call back later." Then hung up. Annoyance taken care of.

Dad looked at me and shook his head. "You probably shouldn't have done that."

Mom just smiled at my "Mabel" moment.

13
The Walk

After my Grandma Nelson died, my parents usually hosted Grandpa for Sunday dinners. That, of course, is lunch for you urbanites. Our evening meal was supper.

When Sunday school was finished at 11 a.m., I would walk the two blocks to his house and wait for Dad to pick both of us up and drive back to the farm. During the lag time between, Grandpa might greet me with a hello — if I was lucky.

Grandpa was not a conversationalist, to say the least. If you look up "stoic" in the dictionary, most likely his picture would be staring back at you. He made Clint Eastwood look like a gab fest. To be honest, I don't remember him ever giving more than two- or three-word answers to any question.

Dinner was usually roasted chicken or a pork roast — both meats were home grown. The conversation was stiff. Mom and her father were not particularly close, but Mom was always pleasant to her father.

He would greet her with a nod and simply say, "Norma," when he entered the house. Dad and Grandpa seemed to get along fine. My Dad would tell the older gent how the crops were looking and how many calves were added to the herd.

Grandpa still owned the farm, but I don't recall him ever questioning anything or giving advice. He would sit quietly, eat his meal through fits of coughing because his untrimmed white handle-bar mustache tickled and listen to the week's report usually without making a comment.

After the meal, if he felt up to it, Grandpa would go for a walk and survey the farm his father bought in 1886. Grandpa was 16 years old when he, his parents and younger sister moved to Iowa from Strawn, Illinois.

During one of these weekly meals, Mom turned to Grandpa and said, "You know what, Morris? Today is Myron's birthday!"

It was curious, Mom always addressed him by his first name. I don't know if this formality was a leftover of long-forgotten English manners or if it was what he preferred.

Grandpa looked up from his plate, nodded and said, "Same month as mine, that's good." Then he went back to nibbling on his chicken. That was a warm and fuzzy response from that man.

When he was finished, Grandpa slowly rose and started out the door on his weekly inspection. At this time, he was in his mid-80s so he was not moving fast.

I scampered out another door, found my stilts and set out to follow him. It didn't take me long to catch up even with my slow lift-the-left-pole, balance, lift-the-right-pole, balance, maneuver.

Grandpa was shuffling up the driveway to check out the crops across the road when I ambled up along side of him. We walked for a bit then I started chatting.

"Grandpa, guess how old I am?" He shook his head. "I'm 10! We have birthdays in the same month!" He nodded and kept walking, and I kept the one-sided conversation going.

"Mom made me a cake, and we're having ice cream with it. Are you staying for cake? Do you like cake? I bet you like ice cream."

Grandpa stopped and regarded me for a moment. "How do you walk on those things?" he asked, finally noticing the green metal poles I was balancing on.

"Practice," I informed him. "I used to fall off a lot but now I'm pretty good."

Grandpa nodded again, walked to the edge of the road and gazed out over the fields he had helped tend for about 60 years. I pranced around and kept yapping. Maybe Charlie the dog was listening, not sure if Grandpa was or not.

His inspection finished, we headed back to the house. Mom told me later it made for quite an interesting sight — Grandpa poking along, me stabbing away with my stilts with Charlie bringing up the rear.

When we got back to the house, we all sat down for cake and ice cream. Afterwards, when Grandpa was getting ready go back to town, he turned to Mom, gestured toward me and said, "Give the boy something."

Mom looked at bit incredulous, asked him how much, wrote a check on his account for $1 and handed it to me.

It was the first time I'd probably seen a check with my name on it. "Thanks Grandpa," I said in awe, staring at the slip of paper.

I swear Grandpa had a twinkle in his eye and he half smiled. He nodded to Mom and walked out to the car, where Dad was waiting to drive him home.

Mom turned to me and said, "That was a first. He never did that for your brothers." Score one for the chatter box.

Fast forward almost 55 years. While attending a memorial service in my home town, a longtime family friend greeted me with a smile. "You know, you look just like your Grandpa Morris."

I nodded. "Yep, every time I look in the mirror, I see him staring back at me."

14
The Escapee

Needless to say, not everything on the farm goes according to plan. During one of our grab-and-snip sessions (castrations) with the piglets, one little boar made it through the process unscathed.

It may have been the fault of the grabber and holder (me) in identifying the male. The pig was small — a runt — even for being about a week old. Since we couldn't tell what sex it was, the pig escaped the razor blade — for awhile.

After a few weeks had passed since his brothers and male cousins were altered, we noticed the runt was an intact male. He was growing but a bit slower than the others.

Thinking back on it, his sire may have been Larry, my Duroc boar whose brother won a purple at the county fair. See the County Fair story in this collection. Larry also was the smallest one among his litter mates.

As soon as Dad noticed the little boar, he started his attempts to catch the pig. Well, That Runt — as Dad called him — had other plans. He turned out to be a smart escape artist and a quick one at that.

We spent the better part of the summer trying to capture That Runt. We'd separate him from the rest of the herd and try to entice him into a shed. Nope, didn't work.

I tried to sneak up on him during feeding time to grab him. He soon caught on to my tactics and always stayed just far enough away from me.

One day, I got frustrated with That Runt escaping my best efforts to capture him. During feeding time, he was running back and forth in front me, almost daring me to chase him.

I picked up a rock and flung it at him. Well, I hit my target. The rock glanced off his head with a sickly thud and he fell to the ground writhing then lay still.

"Oh no, I killed the little (expletive deleted)," I said to my only witness, Charlie the dog. With a pit in my stomach, I walked over to examine the 40-pound carcass and tried to come up with a story to tell Dad.

I started to lean over to grab its leg and drag it out of the pen when That Runt turned into Lazarus. To my astonishment, it jumped up with a grunt, bolted between my legs and once more escaped to freedom.

After a few more weeks, That Runt started showing more aggressiveness than the more docile barrows (castrated males) and gilts (young females). He successfully fought to be first in line for feed and pretty soon he caught up in size to the other pigs.

Now Dad was more determined than ever to "fix" That Runt. He did not want to get docked for marketing an intact male. Once a boar reaches breeding maturity, he starts to exude a "boar taint," which is not desirable for a meat animal.

Dad took extreme measures to capture That Runt. We herded the rest of the hogs into a different lot, where most would be fed out and taken to market. A few of the nicer looking gilts would be held back and be used for breeding stock.

This left That Runt all by himself in a 10-acre pasture and several small sheds to sleep in. Now, the challenge was on. Dad closed off all but one of the buildings and started to leave feed in the open shed.

Several times Dad would fetch me and we would try to sneak up on That Runt while he was feeding. I have to admit my heart was not in this capture-and-castrate mission.

I was not looking forward to holding down a 60- to 70-pound pig while Dad did "the deed." A few times — I now am a bit ashamed to admit this — I sabotaged our missions by spooking That Runt while we were trying to sneak up on him.

Dad may have suspected he had a traitor in his midst, but he never let on. Sorry, Dad.

But, Dad was determined. One night he did not feed That Runt. Early the next morning, he dropped some feed in the open shed, hid around the side and slammed the door on the hungry escapee. Got him!

Later at breakfast, Dad said, "I need your help when we're done. I caught That Runt. We're going to "take care" of him when we're done eating." Oh crap!

I did not relish the walk to the shed. This was not going to be pleasant for any of us, especially for That Runt. We cornered the pig and pulled him down by his legs. I laid on top of the struggling, squealing beast while Dad tied his front and back legs together.

Dad pulled out a knife which he had sanitized with alcohol and is-sued the order I had been dreading to hear all summer. "Now, hold him still." Oh sure.

I put all my weight on top of That Runt but he still managed to thrash and screeched in my ears during "the procedure." Thankfully, Dad was quick and efficient. He had done this hundreds of times but maybe not on such a large patient.

Dad dabbed some ointment on the wound, sliced off the ropes that held his feet and I rolled off That Runt. I felt like a couple linebackers had piled on top of me. The pig got up a little wobbly and limped into a corner.

We kept him in the shed for a few days to make sure he was healing OK then returned him to the herd to fatten up for market. I was almost sorry that we captured That Runt. He had been a worthy adversary.

Vignette IV. Odeurs de la Ferme

OK, so I thought putting the title in French might class this story up a bit. This also is a "tip of the fedora" to a friend and longtime colleague.

This one's for you Mr. RDC.

The English translation of the title is: Odors of the Farm.

Surprisingly, not every smell emanating from or near the farm is repugnant although there are plenty of those unpleasant ones as well. Farmers and their families deal with living things — plant and animal — and sometimes that entails unpleasant duties.

Besides the occasional noxious fumes of manure and the like, there also are the sweet smells of nature and man. Let's get some of the unpleasant odors out of the way first.

Manure is a fact of life when you have livestock. Pens, lots and buildings need to be cleaned out regularly. This can be an unpleasant job depending on your removal technique.

Since I was the lone man (actually, boy) in the farm's pecking order, I got the nasty duty of cleaning out the small hog sheds in the spring, usually March or April. With pitchfork in hand, I scooped the matted straw as quickly as I could and deposited the bundle in the nearby manure spreader.

This job was particularly unpleasant because a blast of ammonia would assault my senses with every scoop. I often had to stand outside to take a breath of fresh air before getting back to work.

Unfortunately, the smell of death is something you recognized instantly. It usually meant the sad duty of finding some animal that had met an untimely end.

These had to be dealt with in appropriate ways. The smaller animals were burned in an out-of-the way brush pile, and the larger animals were carted off after making a call to the rendering truck.

Actually, the smell that bothered me the most came from the former Farmland packing plant. Even though our farm was about five miles away, once in a while you got a sniff of a reminder that the plant was in operation.

On the flip side, spring served up some of the most-delightful fragrances. We had a small grove of plum trees. The smell of their delicate blossoms mixed with the Sweet Williams and other wild flowers.

My mother kept a yellow rose bush outside the south porch door of our house. It was planted by her mother. She loved to stand at the screen door and drink in their lovely fragrance in early summer.

Even though hay season was not my favorite due to the hot, sweaty work that came with it, I have to admit I like the smell of freshly cut hay. It is a strong, pungent but not unpleasant odor. A whiff of cut hay will trigger a time-travel memory in most ex-farm kids that will take them back to their youth.

Smell also can help alert one to potential danger. Beside the telltale ominous clouds, an oncoming rain storm exudes a distinctive humid odor that can be detected from miles away.

Afterwards, there's nothing like sniffing the cool, fresh air after a summer rain.

The most-pleasant aroma that comes to mind was the smell of my mother's potato soup. This scent was particularly delightful on cold, crisp early winter evenings when I was finishing up chores.

Perhaps this is why I choked up every time I smelled food for a few days after she passed away. Who knew the sense of smell can trigger such fond memories.

15
Country Roads

"This little car means a heck of a lot to me
"I remember the day
"when I chose her over all those old broken junkers
"Thought I could tell
"Underneath a coat of rust she was gold
"No clunker
Just couldn't wait to take her home with me ..."
Lyrics from: "This Car of Mine" by the Beach Boys.

L
ike any 16-year-old, I was thrilled when I got my drivers license. Ah, freedom! Busting up the country gravel roads, kicking up a giant cloud of dust behind me, no more school bus rides. Beware common folk, there's a teenager on a mission zooming past.

Then the reality set in, as in "the law" laid out by Mom and Dad:

1. "You will not drive our car every day to school."

2. "Yes, you have to ride the school bus most days. Don't you look at us like that!"

3. "You can drive when you have special activities or after-school functions."

4. "No driving in the winter unless it's an emergency. We will decide if it's an emergency, not you."

5. "And now for the good news. Yes, you can buy a car, but the rules still apply. Stop jumping around like ..." (I will let you use your imagination what Mom said.)

I got my first car about a month or so after turning 16. Mom and Dad drove me to nearby Aplington and looked over the half-dozen or so used vehicles parked in a grassy area just off the highway. With my limited funds, I chose a '63 Plymouth Belvedere. It was a beige monster that featured an airplane-looking dashboard and push-button shift.

Dad looked it over, haggled with the salesman and got the price down to a respectable $300. Not too shabby for 1968 prices. I drove the beast for only a few months until winter arrived.

Of course, I got it stuck in a snowdrift near a neighbor's place and got towed home by a not-too-happy Dad. The car went into hibernation for the next few months until spring arrived and the roads thawed.

My most embarrassing moment with this car was sliding into a ditch while driving to Sunday school (I'm not joking) on my own for the first time. I had just stopped at a T intersection and noticed the Bartling family right behind me.

With a wicked smile, I stomped on the gas, intending to impress the neighbors with my driving skill. The ill-fated demonstration didn't last long. I promptly fishtailed on the loose gravel out of the turn, lost control and drove right into the ditch.

Myrlyn Sr. parked behind me, got out to make sure I was OK. Nothing was damaged except for my pride. All he said was, "Need a ride home?" I nodded and thanked him. My "whoops" happened only a mile from home.

No one in the four-member family said a word as they delivered me home. Thanks Bartlings for not laughing. Maybe they got it out of their system before I got into the car or saved it for later. No matter, they didn't make an already upset teenager feel any worse.

My Dad, though, had plenty to say as we drove the pickup down to pull the car out. After that misadventure, I developed a healthy respect for the tricky gravel roads and never peeled out while turning into an intersection again.

I drove the car for about a year until repairs became more expensive and irritating. When the push-button transmission failed, that spelled the end for the '63.

Not long after saying goodbye to that set of wheels, I went shopping for my next vehicle. I found a white '64 Chevy Impala that had been fixed up by a father of some friends of mine who lived near Eagle City — a wonderful misnomer of a cluster of houses near a span on the Iowa River. It was in better shape and cleaner than my previous ride, so I plunked down $500 and again had four wheels at my disposal.

The Impala got me through high school and the first couple years of college. I picked up my date for the annual FFA Harvest Ball dance and prom in that white chariot.

My first life-flashing-before-my-eyes moment came while driving the heavy Chevy. I was driving home from school and decided to take a different route because the early spring gravel roads were a sloppy mess from the winter thaw.

I had fishtailed most of the way on the country roads in the morning until I gratefully got to the three-mile stretch of blacktop into town. So, my teenage brain decided going home by the south route made more sense. It didn't.

Driving the south route meant I had to traverse a fairly steep incline on a "soupy" road. Not half way up the incline, I started fishtailing again. For some reason I "gunned" it — irrational teenage male brain again — and found myself sliding toward a steep ditch.

I helplessly gripped the steering wheel in terror as the car slid sideways toward the edge of the embankment. Of course I wasn't wearing a seatbelt. Those were for sissies at the time.

It didn't help that my mishap was taking place within a stone's throw of Cross's Ford, where an ancestor had drowned after slipping off the bridge there. I always had a strange feeling about that place. Oh no, one of Levi Nelson's great-grandsons was coming to join him!

The car mercifully came to rest at the lip of the ditch, pitched at about a 45-degree angle. The only thing that stopped it from toppling into the steep drop was the wall of mud that had plowed up during my slide.

I don't know if it was nature, physics or Great Gramps who had a hand in stopping the car, but I was grateful. I shakily climbed out and reassessed my situation. I could either walk the short mile home on a road with mud ruts up to my knees or hike across a couple neighbors' pastures that adjoined our timber. I chose the scenic route.

Once again, Dad came to my rescue with one of our 1940's-something Case tractors. He stopped lecturing me when he saw how precariously the car was perched at the edge of the ditch.

When my folks decided to buy a new car, they sold me their '67 blue-green Plymouth Belvedere for a reasonable price. They traded in my Impala for their new vehicle. I doubt they got much credit for it, though.

For those reading this, you probably are picking up on a pattern here — two cars, two accidents. I will not hold you in suspense about the third car. Yes, I had another mishap. But, I was much farther from home this time — 1 1/2 miles.

I was coming home from a date during college late at night. Well, technically, it was early in the morning during the Great Blizzard of '73. I did not realize how much it had been snowing or how hard the wind was blowing.

The first three miles on the east-west blacktop road was slippery. I breathed a sigh of relief on the mile drive on the first north-south gravel road. It was snow packed but drivable. Then I turned on the gravel east-west road, and it got rocky right away.

The Plymouth bravely broke through the snow drifts like it was going over speed bumps for about half a mile. But, it kept hitting larger and larger drifts. The car finally bottomed out and jerked to a halt like it had hit a brick wall.

I got out of the car and was blinded almost immediately by the snow, which was pelting me sideways by a gusting wind. Home was more than a mile away so I started walking. I could have or should have stopped at the first farmstead but I still harbored the foolish notion I could walk home.

The next quarter mile was torture. I barely made it to another neighbor's farmstead. Blinded by the snow and about as cold as I've ever been in my life, I tried to find their driveway but failed. I fell in the shallow ditch and trudged out.

When I got to their house, I could not see but found the back door to their porch and started pounding. I struck the door so hard its window shattered. The Warren family woke up at the racket and rescued me.

The family took me inside and wrapped me in blankets. I was shaking badly from the cold and tried to mumble an apology about the window. They pooh-poohed that and made sure their icicle of a young neighbor was fine. After warming up, I was steered toward a couch and gratefully fell asleep.

Thank you Warrens. They benevolently shared their food and a couch with me. We watched the storm rage for another day. On day two, the snow plow finally cleared a path on the roads. Dad came to fetch me and we headed out to pull out yet another car I had gotten stuck.

My Dad was not always the most patient person, especially when working with him, but I don't recall the lectures during his rescues of my cars as being too severe.

In fact, he was surprisingly low-key about them. Perhaps, he was glad all he had to do was tow a car home and not scrape a son off a road.

Each of my three children had minor accidents within the first few weeks of turning 16 when they were driving on their own. Perhaps they were genetically predisposed to get into those mishaps. Maybe it was karma.

Either way, I tried to take their "fender benders" in stride and was glad they were alive to tell me about their "whoopses." It will be interesting to see how they react when their children learn to drive.

16
Play Ball!

Sports were not a priority in my early years. Mom and Dad didn't follow any teams and my three older brothers had left home for military duty and/or college and jobs.

It wasn't until fifth or sixth grade when school friends and television helped inspire my interest in anything that had to do with a ball (baseball, football and basketball). Also, the neighborhood kids started getting big enough to venture out and join in pick-up games.

About the same time, the Brown family moved from town to an acreage just down the road from our farm. Mr. Brown kept the acreage nicely mowed, which made for a nice three-hole practice golf course for him, a perfect 50-yard football field and great areas for pick-up baseball and basketball games. The family also had two sons about the same age as the other neighborhood kids.

I was a couple years older than most of the guys. For the first time in life, I was bigger and faster than most of my playmates. Of course I took full advantage of this, but the younger boys didn't complain — too much.

At times the crew consisted of the following roster, subject to change at a moment's notice or call from a parent looking for their wayward children: One Baer, one Bartling, two Browns, two Hackbarths, sometimes an Ellingson, one or two Kelseys (depending if his little sister played), two Winterses, three Vieths, maybe a Cox and lastly, a smart-aleck Williams kid.

Most of the time, there were plenty of bodies for a decent football or baseball game. Play started out as a fairly civilized affair with touch football if the game was on the Brown property. But, as we grew older and testosterone started to course through our teenage bodies, the play got more physical.

A couple of times, Mr. Brown had to employ his landowner's right and ask the noisy bunch to vacate the premises when play got too rough for his liking.

In his defense, Mr. B was well within his rights to ask us to leave when we strayed from the home field's rules. He finally allowed the football games to evolve into tackle, especially when he joined in.

Having Mr. Brown play with us added a whole new dimension. He now was the biggest and strongest player. It usually took me and a teammate to tackle him.

He was a one-person wrecking crew for the home team, bursting through the line and wiping me out with smack-down tackles. On many a Sunday afternoon, I limped home with more bruises than I knew I had muscles.

One crisp Sunday afternoon, the Brown home team with one or two draftees again was taking on the rag-tag visitors led by yours truly. For once, the score was close. Mr. B and I basically nullified each other, and the other kids were evenly matched.

The game featured a lot of punting out of bounds to keep the ball out of hands of the two biggest players — Mr. B and me. On one perfect drive, my team managed to advance the ball with short passes.

First downs were made by a step count. Ten full strides down field was a first down, which was marked with a stick. Simple rule: If you make it to or past the stick, first down!

I made myself a decoy to occupy Mr. B's attention and got the ball to the younger kids. The visiting heathens got to within 20 yards of the end zone, marked by a solitary oak tree.

Mr. B changed his strategy and locked down our receivers. He trailed the next biggest kid and had his players double team our players.

We were facing a fourth down after three incomplete passes by me, who was failing miserably to emulate the Green Bay Packers' Bart Starr or (substitute the name of a favorite quarterback).

Being too close to punt, we went for it one more time. I rolled out to pass, tried to fake Mr. B out and took off downfield. He closed on me quickly and reached out to bring me down.

When we collided, I twisted away and broke free. I heard a thump when he hit the ground and then heard footsteps behind me. I don't believe I have ever run that fast before or since then. My team went nuts when I passed the goal post, er, oak tree.

Mark B came over to me grinning from ear to ear. "Holy smokes! You got away from him." He then sobered up as a shadow loomed over us. Mr. Brown approached me and in a perfect sportsmanship gesture, congratulated me on a good play.

The victorious scamper didn't come without a price. My arm soon started to throb. Looking down, I saw a large gash with a small stream of blood trickling down. It was well worth the wound.

My backyard football career was not always marked with highlights. One Sunday, the neighborhood "gang" decided to play at the Kelsey place. This game included Chuck and his younger sister, a petite, short, blonde 10 or 12 years old.

I should have sensed trouble when Chuck — the future Reverend Kelsey — showed up in shoulder pads. Not cool, and they hurt when colliding with unprotected shoulders.

The game was going back and forth in typical backyard-ball fashion. The home team got the ball and scored after a couple of plays. Likewise with the visitors.

During one of my team's turns on offense, I took a handoff from whomever was playing QB and headed unimpeded for the end zone, except for one small blonde streak who intercepted me.

I can't do somersaults, but what happened must be what it feels like. Without me even seeing her, young Miss Kelsey cut my legs out from under me with a perfect body block.

I remember seeing the sky zip past my eyes, then I landed with a splat on the ground. Once again, I felt like Charlie Brown (See the Snowball story in this collection).

Roger H, who was on my team, looked down at me and couldn't stop giggling. "Boy, she got you good! I've never seen anyone run you down." Thanks, Roger.

After dusting myself off, I glanced at little sis. She stood with her hands on her hips and stared me down, her lips curled in a sneer. In the huddle for the next play, I told my teammates in no uncertain terms to block her.

OK, now it was time to show what the big boys could do. This time I lined up at QB, faked a pass and took off for the end zone, probably located between two apple trees. I sprinted past everyone, intent on turning on the afterburners and zooming impressively into the end zone.

My plan hit a snag — little sis got me again. Once more, I saw the sky where the ground was supposed to be and crashed hard. Again, good ol' Roger H stood, looking down at me.

He was laughing even harder. "I can't believe a little girl did that to you! You should have seen yourself. Your legs went straight up in the air." I probably responded with a few colorful adjectives.

I got up a bit more slowly and called my teammates over. "I told you guys to block her," I growled. They just shook their heads.

"We can't get to her. She's too fast," said Roger H, who looked at me and shrugged. Another kid not-so-helpfully added, "Fastest girl I've ever seen."

On the next play, I again played QB and rolled out again. Little sis was right there, daring me to run. So, I did the manly thing. I passed the ball to another kid who promptly had his bell rung by Chuck. That Kelsey home-field advantage was impressive.

17
Not a Disney Movie

Warning: This story deals with some of the more unpleasant realities of living on a farm. It might not be for you if you think every animal lives to a ripe old age frolicking in beautifully manicured pastures or that farmers are simply the happy-go-lucky custodians of their land. There is no sentimentality or humor here. I feel this collection of stories would not be an honest reflection of my experiences without telling "the rest of the story," as radio personality Paul Harvey used to say. While farming can be a satisfying business and life-style, harsh decisions must be made from time to time.

Everyone who has grown up on a farm quickly learned no animals live forever. All livestock wind up in the food chain. The days of those cute calves, piglets, lambs, chicks and ducklings were numbered.

That favorite calf a young 4-H member fed, washed, trained to lead, groomed and showed at the county fair was destined to become steaks, ribs, brisket, hamburger and many other delicious pieces of meat.

Tears are a common rite of passage for farm kids the first time they watch an animal they had taken care of for well over a year head to market.

My family raised beef cattle and hogs. We also had chickens and ducks, but those critters were almost always used for our own consumption of eggs and meat. I did not show cattle so I was not overly attached to the calves when they were trucked off.

I was more active with the hogs. I watched as they were farrowed (born) and helped wean, feed and water them. From birth to market, it only took about five or six months for our hogs to reach the size where they would be made into roasts, ham, ribs and every meat lover's favorite — bacon.

Unfortunately, not every animal made it unscathed to its planned destination. This also included domestic animals — dogs and cats. While growing up, I dealt with the deaths of four dogs (two were

123

puppies) and countless cats. Some of the felines were my favorites and others were kittens.

Cats can reproduce quickly. After mating, a female will birth kittens in about two months. The mother cats usually weaned their kittens when they reached two or three months old. This means the mother cat will come into heat and likely will be found by a tom and, voila, — a second batch of kittens in less than a year.

While this might sound delightful for cat lovers, Mother Nature can be unkind. A few times some of our mother cats gave birth in the fall and then abandoned the babies.

Cats have great survival instincts. A mother cat giving birth in the fall would not be able to care for babies in the winter without putting herself in danger of starvation. This instinct forced the mothers to abandon the newborns.

Each time this happened, I tried to reunite the babies with their mothers. I knew the cats well enough to tell when a female whose belly was swollen with babies had given birth.

Sadly, the mothers who gave birth in the fall refused to have anything to do with their litters. Anyone who is familiar with cats knows you cannot force a feline do anything it does not want to do.

Nothing is sadder than hearing the mewling of abandoned newborn kittens. There was no pleasant solution to the situation.

My family was not prepared nor willing to play nurse maid to kittens that late in the year. My mother, being a good farm wife, did not allow animals in the house — with very few exceptions.

Kittens born that late probably would not survive the winter. Saving them only to have them die of starvation or freeze to death would have been even crueler.

So, instead of listening to their cries, I ended their distress as quickly and humanely as possible. This was a sad responsibility. It always left me with a pit in my stomach.

The grim chore also fell to me with livestock in my later teenage years. Since I was the afternoon chore boy, I checked on the welfare of new mother sows and their babies. Unlike the modern facilities used by many hog producers today, our facilities were simple — sheds or barn stalls where the females could form a nest and farrow their litters.

In modern units, the babies have their own space divided off by a partition. This dramatically reduces the death rate of piglets from being stepped on or crushed by their mothers.

Even though it may sound kinder for a sow and her litter to be to-gether in a more-open space, this meant we usually lost a piglet or two from every litter due to sow incidents.

Once in a while, I would discover a piglet with a broken leg or back laying in the straw while its mother and litter mates were feeding out-side. Again, I had to dispatch the critter to end its suffering.

One of the saddest scenes I have witnessed came during chore time when I was checking on a sow giving birth in one of our sheds. Every-thing seemed to be fine.

I watched a piglet being born, wiggle around, squeak and struggle to its feet. Then the sow emitted an eerie growl — a sound I had never heard from a hog — stood up and bit the newborn.

I could not believe my eyes and watched in horror as she birthed another and bit it. Knowing I could not handle an angry sow by myself, I raced off, found Dad and told him what was happening.

We grabbed an old gate and rushed to the shed. Luckily the dis-turbed mother did not charge us as we trapped her in a corner. Dad quickly reinforced the gate to the walls. The sow was able to lay down and birth three more piglets which were saved.

Dad was able to "foster" the survivors to another mother sow by rubbing them on the new mother's belly so milk from her teats squirted onto them, soaking the piglets with her scent. After examining the can-nibal's nest, I choked back tears when I found nine dead babies.

I asked Dad why the sow killed her pigs. He just shook his head. "No one knows. It might be some kind off imbalance or she was in pain and took it out on the babies."

The killer sow was shipped off to market the next day. Thankfully, I never witnessed anything like that again.

One frustrating aspect of living on a farm is dealing with stray ani-mals. It seemed some city folks have the misconception good-natured farmers will take care of unwanted pets.

Sometimes this works out, but most often these animals meet an unpleasant end from being run over by vehicles, killed by other animals, starve or being shot by farmers who are protecting their livestock and pets.

Two stray-dog incidents stand out. Charlie, our white Collie mix, would allow no foreign canines to tread on his territory. In one case, I heard a stray chasing calves in one of our pastures near the house. It was far enough away that Charlie didn't go after the interloper right away.

Seeing the commotion, I gave Charlie the "sic 'em" command. He raced off, intercepted the stranger and — in typical Charlie style — soon had the other dog on the ground with his jaws firmly clamped on the other's throat.

I carried a 12-gauge shotgun with me just in case the stray would not back down. However, I did not need it this time.

At my command, Charlie released his prisoner. I've never seen a dog move so fast. The stray yelped, leaped the fence and ran down the gravel road with his tail between his legs. He kept going until I could no longer see him.

A year or so later another stray dog did not get the hint. I heard a commotion in the hog yard and saw several mother sows defending their litters from a strange Collie, who kept diving at the babies and barking savagely.

Again, I sent Charlie to drive off the intruder. Both dogs wrestled and fought for a bit, then the stranger broke off and ran a short distance away.

Thinking the stray would eventually leave, I called Charlie off the chase. Shortly afterwards, the other dog circled around the barn and attacked a mother hen with chicks. It managed to kill most of the brood before I sent Charlie after it.

One more time, Charlie attacked and drove off the stranger only to have it try to circle back and return to the farmstead.

The stray committed the ultimate sin — it killed some of our animals. Charlie and I gave the other dog plenty of opportunity to escape. I checked Charlie for wounds but saw no serious marks.

Now, the stranger made his fatal mistake. He returned to the yard, growled at Charlie and advanced.

I probably uttered some kind of curse. I looked at Charlie. The scruff on his neck was up. His tail stood straight up. His lips were curled in a fearsome snarl.

One more time, I gave him the "sic 'em" command. He charged the stray, and they locked up in gnashing of teeth.

The stray hadn't learned his lesson. Charlie again flipped his foe over, clamped down on his throat and pinned him to the ground.

I watched the ugly scene for a moment and called Charlie off. The other dog staggered to his feet and snarled. I raised my shotgun, fired and ended it.

I was not angry at the dog I had put down but was filled with disgust at its former owners for taking the coward's way out — dumping it and leaving it up to someone else to deal with.

Two unpleasant but necessary procedures we had to deal with were castrating male piglets and inserting rings in the snouts of sows.

The males have to be "fixed" so they will reach market faster and to eliminate their meat from having boar taint — an unpleasant odor — once they reach puberty, usually about the time they would be sent off to market.

This was usually a two-man job. First, we had to lure the sows out with feed to separate them temporarily from their babies. I would grab a piglet and examine it. The females would be set free to join their mothers.

If it was a male, I'd hold it upside down by its hind legs. Dad would do the snipping with a new razor blade and dab some antiseptic on the wound.

Of course the patient was not a willing participant so I had to hold the struggling and squealing critter still. Then, I'd gently put the new barrow (castrated male) on the ground and let it stumble gingerly to its mother.

If I had my druthers, I would help castrate every other day if I could avoid helping with "ringing" sows. This procedure was done to prevent sows from tearing up the ground in their enclosures while rooting for food. A proficient rooter could dig a hole under a fence and escape if not stopped.

About once a year, Dad would matter of factly tell me over breakfast that we were ringing sows today. I'd just grimace and nod.

Two tools were used for this task — a looper and a clamper. That's what I called them.

The looper was a tube with a heavy gauge loop sticking out one end. The other end had a handle or catch at the other end that enabled the loop to be tightened on its intended target.

The clamper looked like a pliers or wire cutter. Basically a heavy staple was placed in the "jaws" of the tool. Then the clamper could be used to snap the staple into the top part of a sow's snout.

Sounds simple enough, right? Nope, not at all.

With me at 5-foot-8 and 130 pounds and Dad at 5-foot-5 and maybe 120 pounds dripping wet, a pissed-off, 300-pound sow should have been able to smash us aside like a bowling ball taking care of a seven-ten split. Luckily for us, that didn't happen.

After Dad fastened the looper over the sow's snout, we'd back the animal into a corner. He'd then hand me the looper and yell, "Hold her, hold her, don't let go." I'd hold the grunting critter while Dad reached for the clamper in his overalls. He then would snap two staples into the snout.

Yes, I said two. The sows would emit an ear-splitting scream while we worked. Dad worked fast but the squealing was deafening. Thankfully, we'd only ring three or four sows at a time, but it seemed like much more.

When released, the sows would bolt away but seemed none the worse for wear. However, my ears would ring for hours after we finished. Now, perhaps my family and friends can understand why I don't like high-pitched noises.

18
The Great Owl Escapade

It's funny how certain adventures or misadventures stand out in your mind. I can remember one of these incidents very clearly even though it happened roughly 60 years ago. As in the above title, I now call it "The Great Owl Escapade."

My brother Gail loved to hunt. As most farm boys, he was a good shot. But the unfortunate side of his talent was his carefree attitude about shooting at anything that came within his field of vision. This included any good-sized bird or varmint that crossed his path or even the horse statuette weathervane that rested on top of the barn cupola.

Being only five years old or so, I don't recall the reason — if there was one — for my brother's unusual hunting trophy. I'd like to think he bagged a predator that had been snatching chickens and/or kittens from the farmyard. Nevertheless, one day Gail walked out of the timber displaying a great horned owl he had shot.

You have to remember, attitudes about hunting were greatly different in the late- '50s compared with 2017. I have a feeling even if regulations existed at that time prohibiting bagging such a magnificent bird, they would not have stopped my brother. He was met with a hero's welcome by my parents and older brothers. The mentality at the time was it was a good thing whenever a predator was killed.

Gail proudly displayed his kill by holding the bird from wing tip to tip. My brother was about 5-foot-8 inches tall. He had to stretch his arms as wide as he could to show off the wingspread.

At 5 years old, I was terrified of the thing even though it was dead. The owl was about as big as I was!

Every family member, except Mom, got their picture taken with the thing. The photos looked like something out of an old National Geographic with big game hunters gathered around an exotic beast one of them had just bagged.

After the photo session, the owl was spread out on top of the cellar doors, which were outside my downstairs bedroom window at the time. I'm not sure what the plans were for it, but I suspect a visit to the local taxidermist was being discussed. I remember staring at the bird for a long time. So that was the beast that woke me up in the middle of the night with its haunting calls.

It was hard to feel sympathy for the bird. Great horned owls always look like they have a perpetual scowl with the way their feathers form a V-shape around their eyes.

The giant birds are noiseless when they fly. It's an eerie sensation to feel something swoop overhead, look up and see a large bird staring down at you as if sizing you up for a possible meal.

I eventually grew tired of observing the dead terror of the night and went into the house when called for supper. After a while, the excitement of the hunt wore off, and everyone went about their business and later all settled in for the night.

Something or some sound woke me up at dawn the next morning. Everyone who knows me well is keenly aware I am not a morning person. Yes, not a favorable trait for a farm boy. I never had to milk cows in the predawn hours, so I never developed an early internal alarm clock.

Remembering that Mr. Owl was right outside my window, I got up to peer at it out of the bedroom window. To this day, I can still remember the shock of what I saw. In fact, I am getting chills while writing this.

Staring back at me were two of the fiercest large golden eyes I have ever seen. Face to face, the owl and I were only about three to four feet away from each other.

I was mesmerized and terrified. The owl seemed to have me in some kind of hypnotic trance. I could not move or speak. The bird was sitting upright taking stock of its situation. In a classic owl move, it's head swiveled around almost in a 360-degree arc.

The owl turned back to stare at me for another moment, then started hopping toward the timber, which was probably about 50 yards away. I watched in stunned silence as my brother's former trophy made its escape into the underbrush.

After finally regaining my senses and voice, I let out a scream. "The owl's alive! It just hopped back into the timber!"

My yell woke up the household. Mom, Dad and Gail rushed to the window and saw that I was not dreaming or playing a trick. My brother muttered some words I did not understand and rushed outside to look.

A minute or so later, he came back in the house and looked at me dubiously. "What did you do with my owl? Where'd you put it?"

I just looked back at him and shrugged. "It hopped back into the timber. I watched it."

Gail glared at me. "Why didn't you say something?"

I lowered my head shamefully and sniffed: "It was looking at right me! I was scared!"

Dad just shook his head and said, "That thing sure looked dead to me. It laid there for hours without moving. I've never seen such a thing." He looked at my brother. "You going out to look for it?"

Gail looked out the window then studied me some more. That devilish twinkle returned to his eyes. "Nope," he said. He turned back to me. "You sure that really happened." I nodded. "Uh huh, good one," he replied, swatted me softly on the head and went upstairs to get ready to go to work.

"What'd he mean by that?" I asked my parents.

Mom chuckled. "I don't think he believes you, but he's going to let it go. I believe you. I don't think you'd touch that thing." She then left to make breakfast for the family.

Dad stared out the window and repeated himself. "I've never heard of such a thing."

19
Fun in the Sun

Farm work doesn't slow down much in the summer. True, the crops are planted and the livestock have free roam of their pastures and pens. Naturally, summer also heralds some of the hottest jobs invented to torture a farm boy — baling (hay and straw) and walking beans — soybeans to be exact.

Haying starts innocently enough. Dad seeded alfalfa with oats early in the spring. The oats grew fast and acted as a nurse crop for the alfalfa. Then, the oats were combined and the seed stored.

Now, the "fun" began. After the oat stalks dried out, they were baled for straw, which was perfect bedding material for mother sows throughout the year and for the other livestock during winter.

After the straw was baled, the alfalfa eventually took over and then it was time to "put up" hay. Of course, oats and hay baling were done on the hottest days of the year. It sure seemed like it anyway.

The procedure for baling hay and straw is about the same. Both crops need to be cut, usually a one-man job.

Then they are wind-rowed by a tractor rake — another one-man job — that formed it into a row that can be baled. The dry oat stalks can be baled pretty quickly after being raked, but alfalfa needs time to dry and, hopefully, not get rained on.

If the weather cooperated, it was baling time. The baling crew usually consisted of two or three workers — one to drive the tractor that pulls the baler and another one or two lucky souls on the hay rack.

The rack workers pull the bales out and stack them high and tight, hopefully, so the whole pile doesn't tumble in an avalanche that could injure them but more importantly — in some farmers' minds — cause lost time picking up broken bales.

It did not take me long to learn why the old farmers wore long-sleeved shirts and jeans during baling. Straw is especially dusty and the cut stems can leave impressive scratch marks.

I learned this the hard way after wearing a T-shirt when baling straw. When I came back to the farm with the load, I not only was covered in dust — everywhere imaginable — but it looked like I lost a fight with a couple pissed-off cats.

My arms and even neck were full of scratches after heaving and pushing around the straw bales. Lesson learned. Long-sleeved shirt next time and no making fun of the old guys who barely had a scratch on them.

When I got bigger, I often was the solo rack man during baling. Most of the time, it worked out well with Dad driving the tractor and baler and me pitching the bales onto a pile.

Of course, when we got ready to take a load of hay back to the farmstead, Dad would rearrange my handiwork to ensure the pile of bales was snug enough to survive the bumpy ride home. I have to admit, the stacks Dad adjusted never swayed as much on the road as the stacks I loaded alone.

We often had a crew of helpers when putting up hay — two or three guys for baling, one to attach the hay fork during unloading, a tractor driver to pull a stack of six or eight bales into the barn and some poor guy in the barn to stack the bales after the fork released them.

For some reason, neighbor Charlie Myers pulled barn duty — a hot, dusty job. I don't know if he requested it or he just didn't want to do the baling part.

Somehow, Charlie would come out of the barn when a rack was unloaded, looking none the worse for wear, take a swig of water and relax under a shade tree until the next load was ready.

See Fun With Big Wheels in this collection for another description of the bale-unloading system.

If Dad was busy unloading a hay rack, he'd recruit someone else to be the baling driver. One of these helpers was a relative of a family friend. I don't remember his name so I'm going to call him Elmer, a good farmer name.

Elmer actually made baling fun. He was an "old guy" with a dry sense of humor and spouted some of the funniest, homespun descriptions of people and events. During a water break when I was working with neighbor Mark B. on the rack, Elmer spotted a car racing north up the gravel road, leaving behind an impressive cloud of dust.

"Would you look at that guy go!" Elmer exclaimed. "He's going faster than a cut cat with his tail on fire."

Colorful sayings like that kept Mark and I laughing so hard we almost fell off the rack a few times. Elmer liked his water breaks and kept us thoroughly entertained.

Most of the time, baling was done without a hitch. After getting into the rhythm of the bumpy ride on the rack and finding my balance when heaving bales onto the stack, I was fine.

One time, however, I wasn't so lucky. I had just picked up a hay bale and was getting ready to swing it up on the stack when one of the tires on the rack hit a badger hole causing the whole load to bounce.

I lost my footing and fell on the rack with the bale on top of me. Several other bales toppled over and fell on my legs. When Elmer looked back, all he saw was my head sticking out from underneath several bales.

Being the expert driver, he eased the tractor to a slow stop. Stopping with a sudden jerk could have caused even more of the hay pile to collapse. Elmer rushed over and helped pull the bales off me.

It took a few seconds for me to tell him I was OK because I had the wind knocked out of me. When I did speak, I let loose with a litany of pretty unpleasant phrases. Nothing was broken, but I had some nasty bruises.

After regaining my composure, I apologized to Elmer for my language. I had never heard him swear so I assumed he was offended.

Elmer just shook his head. "Thought I lost you when I looked back there. Don't worry about swearing, son. I always say, 'Never trust anyone who doesn't swear. They're probably hiding something.'"

A few minutes after we stopped, Dad drove the pickup to where we were to see what was going on. He had noticed the baler stopped in the middle in the field. Elmer reported what happened.

Dad made sure I was OK. I told him I was fine, just a bit sore.

Elmer then did something very cool. In his soft-spoken, matter-of-fact way, he said, "I think the boy could use a break from baling for awhile."

He and Dad exchanged glances. I was given the keys to the pickup to drive home, and Dad finished my shift on the rack. Thanks, Elmer.

Walking beans has become an obsolete chore these days, thanks to science that has produced highly effective herbicides as well as plants that have been genetically modified to withstand the effects of those chemicals.

When I was growing up in the 1960s and '70s, kids were the weed control of choice. This was a hot job best done in the morning before the scorching sun during July and August made it unbearable to walk the field in the afternoon.

I had my standing orders — pull the grass and cockleburs, chop the thistles. So, as I set out armed with gloves, a wicked-looking corn knife and a pith helmet, I probably looked like I was going on an African safari.

A few older guys ribbed me once in awhile about the pith helmet that Mom insisted I wear. These guys wore no hats or shirts when they baled hay and walked beans. I bet they are on first-name basis with their dermatologist today.

Nothing was more boring than trudging up and down the rows of a bean field and stopping every few yards to whack or pull out an intruding weed. When I was younger, it helped pass the time by pretending I was a knight of King Arthur's Round Table wielding Excalibur and helping to behead enemies of the realm.

A few times, I got carried away with swinging Excalibur and started chopping cockleburs instead of pulling them.

Yes, the cockleburs grew back. Yes, Dad noticed. And, yes, yours truly was sent back to the field, minus his trusty sword, to yank them out of the ground.

Did I eventually learn my lesson to pull out those pesky weeds? Perhaps.

20
Adventures on No. 9

It's 7:40 a.m. and a certain bleary-eyed farm boy is staring out the southeast corner living room window, searching the "east road" for sign of the big yellow monster that was coming to swallow him up.

That was my daily routine for 10 to 11 years during the school year — scanning the horizon, waiting for the cloud of dust that signaled No. 9 would be pulling into our driveway.

My first memory of boarding the school bus was one winter day when I was in kindergarten. The bus had just pulled in and Mom got me started trudging across the snow drifts in our yard. I was bundled to the max, possibly looking akin to the Randy character, Ralphie's little brother, in the movie, "A Christmas Story."

About half way across the yard, ker-plop. I sunk into a drift up to my head. All I remember are the muted sounds of my mother yelling. Then, seconds later, a hand grabbed me by the collar, scooped me out of the drift and plunked me down in the aisle of the bus.

My brother, Gail, bolted out of the house, charged through the drifts and rescued his little brother. His plopping of me onto the bus was a bit rough. I kind of swayed back and forth like I was going to tip over.

Some older girls took pity on me and helped brush the snow off. Now, that wasn't so bad.

Another early memory was the time when one of the older boys got kicked off the bus in mid route for being mouthy. The driver at time was Mr. V, and he didn't take back talk from anyone. That impressed upon me the wisdom of not testing the driver's patience.

Oftentimes, Mom would be my sentinel and give me the count-down when she saw the bus crest the hill past the Walthall place.

"You've got two minutes!" she'd call, adding, "Hurry up with your breakfast," or "You'd better be done in the bathroom!" Whatever was appropriate.

141

If I was on time and ready to go (people who know me will find that statement quite funny and hard to believe), which was rare, I would meet good ol' No. 9 at the driveway entrance. Unfortunately, many (OK, OK, most) times, I would blast out the porch door and race for the bus as it was pulling into the lane.

The driver was Mr. H, our neighbor. He was on a tight schedule. I'm not exactly sure, but I think he gave his passengers about 10 seconds before he tooted the horn.

The countdown was on if you did not show after the second blast of the horn. Mr. H would back out of the driveway and continue his route. Woe be to the tardy kid whose unhappy parents had to drive him or her to school.

During the times I could not make the bus — usually sick or just running late — Mom would call the Bartlings and ask them to let Mr. H know that I would be a no-show. They were about a half mile away just to the east and out of sight behind the Walthalls.

If Mr. H had already picked up the Bartlings, Mom would wave out the door to let him know he wouldn't have to put up with the Williams kid this time. He probably enjoyed those days.

Toward the end of my bus-riding career, I walked the short distance to the East Road's T-intersection. This saved Mr. H the time and trouble of pulling in and backing out of our driveway. Hopefully, this made up for some of my antics Mr. H had to put up with over the years.

Our school bus and probably most others had its pecking order. The younger you were, the closer to the front you sat.

Getting to the back seat of the bus was the goal of every kid — the throne, the seat of power. Of course, the older youngsters sat in the back and the most senior kid got to determine who sat beside him or her across the aisle. Ahh, the sweet taste of power.

As luck would have it, I was the oldest boy on the bus my sophomore and junior years. Do not worry, I was a benevolent dictator. At least, that's how I remember it.

In the mornings, I would head to the back of the bus. If the seat was occupied by some younger kids, they would scramble to relocate.

I actually never used any bullying tactics, it was just the natural order. Once in a while some of the younger kids refused to move.

That was OK, I'd sit in the next seat or two away. Usually, after a stop or two later, the back-seat interlopers would find a reason to move or would scoot over and offer me a spot.

I relinquished the back seat on the trip home in the fall because all the dust from the gravel roads settled back there. The buses were not air conditioned. If we wanted fresh air, windows could be opened half way. Thank goodness the heater worked in the winter.

It was actually during the times of sitting in the middle of the bus when more mischief broke out. This was where I honed my rubber-band-shooting abilities.

We'd wait until Mr. H would take his eyes off the spy mirror when turning or stopping and let our missiles fly. If he caught the perpetrators in the act, it meant finishing the ride in the front seat.

Oh, the embarrassment! This was something akin to being sentenced to the stocks during Pilgrim times.

Of course, I was the one of the chief missile launchers. I loved to smack a rubber band off the back of a kid's head, then look as innocent as possible while the target sought his attacker.

Former passengers of No. 9, I apologize for using many of you as targets. Some of you got even with me once in a while with return fire. Good shot. I'm sure I deserved it.

One time, a missile I launched missed its target — I think the kid moved — and bounced off the inside of the windshield. Mr. H slammed on the brakes and pulled the bus over. Oh crap, I was sure this was my getting kicked-off-the-bus moment.

Every kid was very somber during Mr. H's justified tirade. He declared a no-rubber-band-or-paper-wad-shooting zone. The next perpetrator would GET KICKED OFF THE BUS!

To their merit, none of my fellow passengers ratted me out. No missiles were launched for at least two or three weeks after that.

Another time, Mr. H's son, Roger, and I were giving each other a hard time. It wasn't a scuffle at all, more like good-natured poking back and forth.

Roger was sitting ahead of me and made the mistake of turning around to probably defend himself from whatever I was doing to him. I pinned his arms to the back of his seat and sort of hung him in place.

However, when Mr. H looked in the spy mirror, it looked like Roger, a stocky kid, was pounding on me when, in fact, he was quite helpless. At the next stop, Mr. H gave his son a lecture and sent him to the front seat.

Sorry, Roger, that was on me.

My fellow passengers and I did settle down during inclement weather, be it a thunderstorm or blizzard. Most of us had sense enough to let Mr. H concentrate and get us home safely.

I did get my just reward one time. One of my buddies had just zinged a rubber band off my ear. I turned around to retaliate and was caught in mid draw by Mr. H.

The bus was very quiet when I shuffled up to the front seat. Mr. H told me how disappointed he was in me and that, as an older boy, I should set a better example for my minions (my words not his).

I thought I had done that because I taught most of the kids how to shoot rubber bands. I didn't dare tell him that.

Good point, Mr. H. Rowdy activity on the bus was drastically reduced after that.

During my senior year, I drove to school most days. A new pecking order was established, except for those rare days when the former head honcho needed a ride and claimed his rightful place in the back seat.

Vignette V. Troubled Waters

Our farm was only about a half mile from the Iowa River. So, of course, you must think I led a Tom Sawyer-like existence of grabbing a fishing pole when bored and spent lazy summer afternoons snoozing under a shade tree while my bobber dipped up and down in the current.

Nope, not even close. I think the first time I went fishing was with a friend's family when I was in fourth or fifth grade.

I seem to have been genetically predisposed to distrust water, particularly the Iowa River. My family has a sad history with that 320-mile-long waterway that meanders through much of Central Iowa and eventually empties into the Mississippi.

Ever since I was very small, my family instilled a fear of water in me. Why? The river claimed the lives of my maternal great-grandfather and possibly paternal grandfather. Not good karma there.

My great-grandfather Levi Nelson was leading a horse and buggy across a small bridge during a nighttime rain storm at Cross's Ford when he slipped and fell into the water. The tragedy was made even sadder, if that was possible, because he was leading the carriage carrying his son and his bride (my grandfather and grandmother) back home after their wedding.

The accident took place at the closest point the river was to our family farm, only a half mile away. That would have been the most accessible spot for me to have gone fishing.

After retiring from the farm to a house in nearby Iowa Falls, Grandpa Warren Williams went for one of his early evening walks one day but did not return home. His body was found in the river the next day. To be fair, it is not known if he also slipped and fell into the water or had a heart attack and ended up in the water.

So, with this history looming over me, Mom reluctantly agreed to enroll me in swimming lessons at the Iowa Falls pool. I took lessons for only one season.

It took me most of the summer to learn how to face float. I hated to put my face in the water. However, it only took me a few days to do the back float. Why? Because I did not have to put my face in the water — simple. I was told that was the opposite learning curve for most kids. Imagine that.

Even my children seemed slow to take to water and never liked water in their faces, either. They did take swimming lessons, though, and got proficient enough so at least they would not drown.

One time, a well-meaning relative was helping bathe one of my grandsons when he was a toddler. To speed things along, she dumped a glass of water on his head. He let out a scream that sent my daughter running to see what happened.

After finding out what happened, my daughter explained that he didn't like water in his face. Imagine that.

He and his sister now are taking swimming lessons and are learning to dip their heads into the water. Maybe the curse is broken.

21
The East Road Gang

About the time I reached 14 years old, I started jumping onto my one-speed, red Monark bicycle to explore the countryside and visit my school-bus buddies. Pretty soon, there were about six of us racing up and down the gravel roads between "old Highway 20" and Eagle City.

One stretch of road that was a particularly favorite route was simply called the "East Road." When returning home, that road made the trip easier and fun due to its gentle slope.

If a rider got up a good head of steam when cresting the hill at the old Walthall place, he could coast for over a tenth of a mile or so before having to return to pedaling. This was much appreciated after huffing and puffing for three to four miles coming and going during that day's adventure.

Most of these rides usually were organized around backyard baseball or football games, which were were hosted by various neighbors or at Eagle City Park. (More about these games is described in the Play Ball story in this collection.)

After a few phone calls back and forth, our little group of pedal pushers — yes, pun intended — would descend on the agreed-upon site, beat up on each other — if it was football — then limp, ride or walk our bikes back home.

At one time, I had intended to ride my pony to some of these activities, but she had other ideas. (See Snowball, Pony From Hell in this collection.)

The East Road actually was only about a mile long. It eventually curved to the north and connected to old Highway 20. Or, you could turn south at the "T" and head toward Eagle City, a cluster of houses on the other side of the Iowa River.

Funny, but my group of friends and I never ventured over the bridge to explore where the road past Eagle City ended up. Perhaps it was the idea we might run into some kids from Eldora. Heaven forbid!

Our gang of intrepid explorers started venturing farther and farther from home. One time, we followed the East Road and continued on when it curved north. We eventually came to the stop sign at the intersection of the highway.

Going back south would only take us home. But, a few miles north was the grain facility at the long defunct village of Macy. Not wanting to go home, we kept going north to check out what Macy had to offer for a few inquisitive boys.

A couple more miles of pedaling brought us to Macy. The grain-storage company and a nearby house or two were the only things left of the town.

We peeked into the office and discovered a welcome sight to thirsty travelers — a pop machine.

I found a dollar bill in my jeans pocket and got change for it. Not realizing I was acting as a Socialist, I distributed my wealth amongst my comrades. We plunked in our dimes and grabbed our favorite pops. Yes, Iowans say "pop."

My Nesbitt's orange never tasted so good after the long ride in the summer heat. My companions enjoyed their grape, Squirt and root beers.

Even though it was quite a trek from where we started out, our "East Road Gang" made it back to Macy a few more times that summer. The only reward for our efforts was pulling the dime bottles out of that old pop machine, but it was worth it.

During one bike jaunt when we were coming home down the East Road, one of my buddies and I thought a game of "chicken" was a good idea. For those of you who are made up of kinder sensibilities, the game of chicken consists of two usually testosterone-laced guys riding or driving straight at each other to see who "chickened out" and pulled to the side.

I agreed to my friend's challenge because he always swerved at the last second when we previously challenged each other and had to wear the chicken title. Yes, we had done this before. We were teenage boys. Need I say more?

We faced each other from about twenty yards away. On the count of three, we charged each other like jousting knights of old. Since we had no horses, the only sound was that of the gravel being displaced by our bike wheels.

My buddy was hunkered down on his banana-seat bike, a frown creasing his lips. At the last second, I realized he was not going to swerve. He must have been tired of being "the chicken."

I tried to avoid him, but it was too late. My handlebars rammed into his shoulder. His handlebars gouged into my side. We collided in a crash of metal. Both of us spun out and skidded body first onto the gravel road.

If you've ever seen the Peanuts comic strip when Charlie Brown gets knocked off the pitcher's mound after being hit by a line drive, you can imagine the scene on the East Road that day.

I lay on the edge of road with my bike on top of me. Looking up, I heard my pal moan but only saw his bike tipped over backwards. Pretty soon a head popped out of the ditch. He crawled out, his glasses askew and blood trickling down his nose.

We suffered nothing worse than a few cuts and bumps. Our bikes were in worse shape than we were. My pal's handlebars were twisted halfway around his bike. My seat was spun backwards.

He looked at me and said the obvious: "That hurt." I nodded in agreement and dried off the cuts on my hand and arms.

When we got about halfway home, my pal turned and said, "That was fun. Let's do it again!"

I looked at him in disbelief, shook my head and said, "Nope."

An evil smile flashed on his face. "Then, that means you're chicken."

It didn't take long for me to consider the ramifications of the title along with the pain of our recent collision. "OK, I'm chicken."

He looked at me and crowed, "I won!" I nodded, then we both limped home to tend to our wounds and fix our bikes.

22
Hunting

For many farmers and their families, hunting is just another sport. It is easily accessible when you live on the land. All my family had to do was grab a rifle or shotgun and patrol our property looking for a variety of game: pheasants, rabbits, deer, grouse, fox, raccoons, squirrels, ducks, geese, badgers or woodchucks.

I can barely remember not having a gun handy. My first weapons lesson was at age 6. I heard a pop-pop-pop coming from my brother Gail's room.

Gail and brother Roger were supposed to have been babysitting me. The sound interrupted whatever TV show I was watching at the time — either Howdy Doody or The Floppy Show with Dwayne Ellett. I went to investigate.

Thinking he was throwing firecrackers out the window, I traipsed up the high wooden stairs and peeked into his room. He was shooting at cans on the ground. Seeing he had company, Gail gestured for me to see what he was up to.

After a quick lesson on the .22 rifle — "Put the stock snug to your shoulder, peer down the barrel, point the sight at your target and squeeze the trigger." — I fired my first weapon. Guess what? I actually hit the can, which brought hoots of encouragement from both brothers.

I missed my next several shots so it must have been beginner's luck. It also was the first time I kept a secret from Mom.

"You'd probably better not tell Mom," Gail advised. "I'm sure she thinks you're too little to handle a gun." I nodded solemnly, and we three brothers swore an oath of secrecy.

Of course, Mom eventually found out, probably from me spilling the beans. This led to a very lively lecture to my brothers about future babysitting duties and the edict of keeping guns away from a 6 year old.

However, the damage was done. I had tasted the thrill of the hunt — if shooting at a tin can out of a bedroom window counts.

At age 8, I got a Daisy Winchester replica BB gun for my birthday. I probably acted a bit like the Ralphie character in the Christmas Story movie when he opened the package and saw his Red Ryder BB gun. Dad gave me permission to shoot pigeons and other small critters but said to leave the livestock alone.

I soon became the barn pigeons' worst nightmare, much to the delight of the mother cats when I would fling one of my trophies their way for a meal. The pigeons soon learned to take flight quickly when they saw me climbing the ladder into the hay loft.

This turned into a game of stealth with me sneaking slowly into the barn and quickly taking aim at one of those fat birds. Don't feel too sorry for the pigeons. Most of the time they fluttered to safety before I could draw a bead on them.

A month or so after getting my BB gun, I got my first in-your-face safety lesson. Brother Roger was leaving to drive into town for work when he walked past me on the way to his car.

We exchanged pleasantries (most likely brotherly insults), and he got into his car and started to drive away. For some reason, the ornery kid in me decided to aim at his back window and take a shot.

Not sure how I hit a moving car but I did. Bad decision and bad luck for me.

I've never seen a car back up so fast and do a 180-degree turn. Roger got out and let me know very loudly what a stupid thing I had done. It was the first time he had yelled at me like that. Lesson learned.

Mom looked out the screen door and saw the brothers were settling the dispute on their own. She simply said, "I think we need to put your BB gun away for awhile." A justifiable sentence.

However, I would receive one more emphatic lesson from another brother a few years later. At age 11, after no more shooting-at-things-I-shouldn't incidents, I got a .22 bolt-action, single-shot rifle for my birthday.

Now rabbits, squirrels and other pesky varmints became targets. I became pretty proficient on fall afternoons at bagging squirrels. Again, the mother cats were happy to eat what I shot.

The next summer, my oldest brother, Wes (given name, Neville), and I agreed to go target shooting during one of his visits home. He lived in Utah with his family so it was a rare opportunity to do something with him.

We took an old bucket, filled it with tin cans and headed toward the edge of the timber where we would set up our target practice. Wes put the bucket down, pulled a couple cans out and walked 10 feet or so to set up the targets.

Once again, the ornery kid in me decided to unleash my idea of fun. I aimed my .22 at the bucket and fired. For some reason, I thought it would be funny to put a hole in a few cans before we started.

A startled Wes jumped away, realized I shot at something very close to him and proceeded to give me another very loud lesson in gun safety. It was the first time he also had yelled at me like that. It was justified. Lesson learned, again.

By the time I was 13 or 14, I was allowed to use our shotguns. Dad owned a five-shot, pump-action 12-gauge and a single-shot .410.

The .410 barely looked bigger than a rifle. It didn't have much range and its shells didn't have much spread. A shotgun shell contains a load of tiny pellets that explode out the barrel when the gun is fired. Various types of shells have different patterns or spreads when they are fired.

I soon found out the .410 was really good for shooting pigeons off the barn roof. It also was very efficient for blasting squirrels out of trees. But, that was hardly fair.

All you had to do was shoot close to where the squirrel was clinging to a branch to bring it down. Also, after a shotgun was fired, every squirrel within a half mile would take cover for hours.

Dad usually reserved the 12-gauge for himself. He liked to hunt groundhogs and badgers. Both large varmints can be a pest on a farm.

Groundhogs, which can be the size of a small dog, like to dig under buildings which eventually could undermine a foundation. Badgers were more solitary but also dug large holes in fields, which could damage equipment when a tire rolled into one.

As I got older, I was allowed to use the big shotgun. On late fall or early winter days, a couple buddies from town liked to visit to hunt pheasants. We would traipse through my family's fields in hopes of bagging one of those elusive birds.

We were skunked more often than we got a shot off. However, there's something very fulfilling about hunting with friends, even though the only thing you come home with is cold toes.

Three memorable hunting experiences stand out in my mind — stalking raccoons at night, trying to sneak up on Canada geese and lying in wait for a deer herd.

I tried to hunt raccoons only once. My buddy, George I., had a hound that could trail the tricky creatures and tree them. One crisp fall night under a full moon, George showed up with his dog and off we went into the timber.

George and I were packing shotguns and flashlights. The plan was the dog would tree a raccoon, we would use the flashlight to spot the eye glow and shoot it. The raccoons had other ideas. They were nowhere to be found.

We stomped around in the dark woods for a few hours. George's dog tried to pick up a scent but was unsuccessful that night. It actually was fun being out at that hour, telling stories and having a good time.

The only thing we accomplished was keeping me from getting injured. George and I were shuffling along when a hand reached out, grabbed my collar and pulled me back. I was only a step away from tumbling into a fairly deep ravine. Thanks, George. I owe you one.

Brother Gail loved to hunt. One fall day, we spotted some Canada geese on our farm pond. We grabbed our shotguns and drove into a cornfield and parked far enough away so as not to spook the geese.

We then crept through harvested corn stalks on our hands and knees to where we could see the geese. Now, we dropped to the classic Army crawl and started to inch our way closer.

Gail had been in the Army. After a few minutes of this caterpillar pace, he had had enough. With a whoop, he leaped to his feet, jumped over me and charged the geese Rambo style, firing his shotgun from his hip. I didn't get a shot off.

All I remember is two legs sailing over my head, the sound of boom, boom, boom, and the geese honking in fright and flying away unscathed. I stood up and shook my head.

Gail watched our prey escape, turned and walked over to me. "Well, that didn't work," he said with his classic sly grin.

When we got back home, Dad came over to see how many of the birds we had dropped.

"What?" he said, when he discovered we had been skunked. Williams boys were supposed to be sharpshooters don't you know. "I counted at least four shots. You missed them all?"

Gail just shrugged. I looked at my brother then at Dad, also shrugged and said, "Something must have spooked them."

The same brother also was at the scene of my most infamous hunting experience. Dad had planted soybeans into what had been a 10-acre pasture just south of our house.

After harvest, a herd of deer would come out at dusk to forage under a large oak tree that sheltered a patch of unharvested beans. The combine couldn't get close enough to the tree to get to the plants.

We counted more than 20 deer one night. So, of course, a hunt was planned.

An hour or so before dusk, I hunkered down with one of Gail's guns in an empty shed very close to where the deer would emerge. Dad and Gail were spread out in the trees behind me.

I was given the honor of taking the first shot. Never having bagged a deer or hunted one, I was excited about the opportunity.

At dusk, the deer herd started emerging from the timber. It took little effort for them to hop the fence and head for the tree which sheltered the beans. Four or five does walked past me.

I didn't shoot. I wanted the big buck we had seen. Not long after, here he came. He practically stepped over the fence and slowly made his way toward me. When he was parallel with where I was hiding, I slowly stuck out the gun, peered down the sight on the barrel and followed him as he walked past.

He was a magnificent, regal buck with maybe 8- or 10-point antlers. I sighted on him perfectly but couldn't bring myself to shoot such a beautiful animal.

After a few seconds, a shot rang out from behind me. A young doe fell dead in her tracks as the rest of the herd charged back into the timber.

Gail and Dad walked up to me. "What happened? Gun jam on you?" Dad asked.

I looked down at the ground and shrugged, waiting to be berated for my failure.

"I counted to 10 then shot that doe. She'll be good eating," Gail said. He glanced at me then strode over to admire his kill.

Dad patted my shoulder. "That's OK, you must have gotten 'buck fever.' Happens to everybody." Nothing else was said.

He joined Gail, and they planned the butchering procedure. My brother was right. The venison from that doe was delicious.

23
Farm Sale

During the summer of my 20th year, I witnessed the end of an era. Over breakfast one August day, Dad asked if I could help with something on a Saturday in two weeks.

I paused and looked up. His voice was soft and a bit hoarse. He and Mom were both looking down at their plates, not making eye contact — very unusual. Something was wrong.

"Sure, what's going on? Is everything OK?"

Dad nodded. "We're having a farm sale. I need you home to help."

I gasped. "What!? We're selling the farm?"

"No, no, just most of the equipment and a lot of the tools," Dad reassuringly explained. "We're keeping the farm. We'll rent out the crop ground."

Mom looked at me with a half smile. "Your father is turning 65 next year, and we need to sell off some of our things before he fully retires."

I sat there, stunned, as the realization swept over me. This was a watershed moment. Dad was leaving farming with no heirs stepping forward to take over.

My three older brothers had all gone their separate ways. Two of them were married and were raising families. I was headed back to college with no intention of returning to the farm.

In fairness, brother Gail farmed the land for a while. He and his family lived in town and he had a full-time job.

My brother gave it a valiant effort for a couple years but couldn't make it work in the 1970s with only about 160 acres of cropland and no livestock. Dad sold off all the livestock several years before when his last chore boy — me — started college.

Our family was moving on. My mother was an only child so the Nelson side was done, and now our branch of the Williams family was cashing it in. Only one Williams was left farming, a cousin about 10 miles away.

For generations, as far as we knew, the Nelsons and Williamses were farmers. Both sides immigrated to the United States as farmers. The Nelsons had been in this country for 10 generations and the Williamses probably a generation or two later.

While working for a farm magazine, I once interviewed a farmer in the country of Luxembourg. I asked him how long his family had farmed.

He listened to the interpreter and held up four fingers. She told me, "They have lived in this place for four generations."

I shook my head and tried to clarify my question: "How long has your family been farmers?"

He looked at me, then waved a hand toward his fields. "Fir emmer." The translator smiled. "Forever."

Same with my family.

The day of the sale was surreal. Dad had gathered many of his better tools and put them on a hay rack. The "big" tractor, a yellow late-60s Case, was parked nearby. The baler, planter, plow, hay rake, corn picker and a few other small implements were on display in another part of our large front yard, which stretched to the road.

People started coming an hour before the 9 a.m. auction start time to look over the goods. Cars lined the road to the north and south of our driveway. I had never seen so many people swarming around the farm.

My unenviable job was to watch the hay rack to make sure no one attempted a "five-fingered discount." I was given a couple of names to watch for and ordered to follow them around or at least be visible to keep everyone honest. Oh, brother.

The auctioneer began promptly at 9. Like a good salesman, he extolled Dad's work ethic, honesty and emphasized how well he cared for his equipment. In all honesty, a lot of what he said was true, but most of Dad's equipment was aging out.

People were there for bargains. The auctioneer and Dad knew it. Dad was no stranger to auctions. He loved to attend Saturday night sales in town. He knew how the game was played.

To my relief, the auctioneer started with the small stuff, which I was supposed to be guarding with my life. He started his rapid, sing-song chant.

"We've got a box of wrenches here folks, good solid steel. What do you give me? Do I hear five dollars? Five dollars, five dollars, five dollars. Oh, come on folks, this is worth four times that. You, there, Floyd (not his real name). You've been eyeing that box, give me a dollar!"

Floyd nodded, and the auction was on its way. I don't remember for sure, but I think the auctioneer finally milked four dollars out of Floyd for the wrenches.

Thankfully, the bidding picked up for the other small stuff and soon I was off the hook for guard duty. The auctioneer's voice grew more dramatic and the crescendo increased with the large equipment, which drew the interest of most of the crowd.

I stood back and watched the equipment I had worked with, cussed at and driven up and down the roads to our fields be judged, bought and handed over to strangers. Two of my friends from a few miles away peered out of a second-story barn window to get a better view of the unfolding drama.

The auctioneer saved the best for last — the big tractor. He knew how to keep the crowd motivated. Dad sat in the seat. He looked like he was saying goodbye to his best friend.

"How many hours do you have on that tractor?" the auctioneer asked. Dad told him a number, which sounded a bit low to me, but I kept my mouth shut and made eye contact with no one.

This is when the auction slid into slow motion for me. I could see Dad was tearing up as he looked away from the action. A crowd gathered around the tractor. They were quiet and respectful.

The only sound was the auctioneer crying out a number and an occasional "yep" called out from the crowd. I watched for a few minutes more, turned away and walked into the house.

Curiously, Mom did not watch any of the sale. "How are things going out there?" she asked.

"OK," I said with a shrug. "They're selling the tractor now." Mom just nodded and continued to make supper. She was unusually quiet.

I slumped into a chair and tried to take my mind off what was happening outside. It was hard to watch the end of an era.

24
Saying Goodbye

Note: The events in this story took place in 1997.

The pen in my hand paused over a document I was supposed to sign. For the past eight months, I had been prepared for this act, but it was harder to do than I imagined.

My three brothers and I were selling the tillable portion of our family farm — 162 acres — in Hardin County, Iowa. An era of our family history officially was being closed. After more than 100 years, we no longer would be involved in farming that piece of ground six miles southeast of Iowa Falls.

In truth, we had not actively farmed for several years. A renter and family friend had capably taken care of things. He made sure the farmland produced what it had for decades — corn and soybeans.

My mother's death in March sealed our decision to sell. The farm had been her family's, the Nelsons. She was born in the farmhouse across the road, where the remaining 40 acres of our property were located.

Our great-grandfather, grandfather, father and my brother, Gail, all took their turns plowing, haying, sowing oats, planting, harvesting and pasturing a small beef herd — and milk herd in earlier years — on that quarter.

As I looked at that paper, it felt like I was throwing away a part of me. I was taking leave of an old friend. Memories came flooding back — painful ones, happy ones.

There were times, I admit, when I was not always thrilled with those acres, such as haying during the hottest day of the year, picking rocks out of the field when I would have preferred to be playing ball, herding the cows back to the barn while keeping an eye on a cantankerous bull.

The tract also provided good times. It was ideal hunting ground for pheasant, rabbits, fox, badger, ducks and geese.

Many times on a crisp fall day, I crept through corn stalks trying to get close enough to shoot at waterfowl on our farm pond, which now would be labeled a wetland. They often heard me coming and escaped. Once in a while, I brought home dinner.

That land had always been there, as far as I was concerned. I was 2 years old when my family moved to the home place after my grandparents retired to town.

My mother could look out the dining room or living room windows to survey the whole area. She knew where we were when we were across the road.

Pangs of guilt swept through me as I signed the legal paper. Somehow I felt like I was letting my ancestors down. They had scrimped and sacrificed at times to hang on to that farm.

My Grandfather Nelson refused to lose the farm during the Depression. He made small payments to retain possession, though the bank refused to let his family live there. A few years later, they were back on the place.

My paternal grandparents were not so lucky, losing their farm that bordered our farmstead just to the south.

Our land evolved the same way as many other farms did in our area of North Central Iowa. The pond was tiled out, the cows sold and the virgin pasture plowed up to make room for more crops in the late-'60s.

Severing ties with the farmland made me feel like I also was saying farewell to neighbors and other friends I had known all my life. I had lived away from the farm for 22 years, at the signing, but every time I came home, many of these folks were still there — a rare testament to the longevity and generational commitment to the land.

Some of their names have since disappeared from the mailboxes. But their names will live in my memory forever: Bartling, Borchers, Brown, Chaplin/Diemer, Cox, Hackbarth, Ites, Kelsey, Mossman, Myers, Oppold, Rush, Schafer, Thorpe, Walthall, Warmbier, Warren, Willems and Winters.

Many of these families have worked their farms for two and three generations. Even though my family no longer farmed, a Williams was part of the neighborhood for a while.

For a few years, my brother, Roger, lived on the remaining 20-acre farmstead, which included the barns and out buildings. Roger later sold the farmstead and returned to his beloved West Coast, where he lived until his death in 2014.

Through the years, one rule remained true — if you took care of the land, it provided for you. As the sale was completed, the land provided for my brothers and me one last time.

The happy part concerning the sale was the land transferred to the care of a neighbor whose family has been in the area as long as mine. At the time, they were welcoming a son into their operation. It is gratifying to see another generation continue the tradition.

I pray they will respect the land as has my family. If they care for it, the land will provide for them.

Made in the USA
Middletown, DE
15 August 2019